About Ordinary Folks Who Said We Can: & They Did

Focus On Renewal : the McKees Rocks, Pennsylvania Story

by

Paulette G. Honeygosky, vsc

1663 Liberty Drive, Suite 200
Bloomington, Indiana 47403
(800) 839-8640
www.AuthorHouse.com

© 2004 Paulette G. Honeygosky, vsc
All Rights Reserved.

No part of this book may be reproduced, stored in a retrieval system, or transmitted by any means without the written permission of the author.

First published by AuthorHouse 10/21/04

ISBN: 1-4208-0339-5 (sc)

Printed in the United States of America
Bloomington, Indiana

This book is printed on acid-free paper.

*dedicated to the memory of
Cardinal John Wright
who prophetically challenged us,
then and now, "to do" the gospel;
"to put faith into practice"
in the Neighborhood in which we live,*

*and to the memory of
Dr. Bruce Bender,
who served so many, so well
at the F.O.R. Family Health Center;
who died too young; too soon,*

*and to
the many volunteers and professionals,
who continue to work side by side,
having done so now for more than three decades,
to improve the
quality of life
of the poor and the elderly
in the Neighborhood of Sto-Rox*

*… of each it can be said, "they went about
doing good for each other "….*

Table of Contents

PREFACE..ix

THE TOWN'S INITIAL STRUGGLE FOR FREEDOM: 1969 - 1973 1

HOW THE F.O.R. STO-ROX NEIGHBORHOOD CORPORATION WAS CREATED... 18

PROBLEM SOLVING IN THE NEIGHBORHOOD................................. 32

THE HEALTH CENTER STORY 33

THE AMBULANCE STORY 43

THE TOWN'S GROWING PAINS May, '72 - March, '73...................................... 54

PEOPLE OF STO-ROX EVER MORE IN CHARGE 74

THE TOWN'S NATURAL LEADERS TAKE OVER, AS THE HOME RULE QUESTION SURFACES 90

AN OPEN-ENDED DEVELOPMENT PROCESS: 1974 - 2004...................... 106

PEOPLE GREW TALL IN THE STRUGGLE..110

F.O.R. STAFF DOCTORS VISITING WITH THE ELDERLY HOMEBOUND IN THE NEIGHBORHOOD 125

A WORD ABOUT HUMANITY IN PROCESS; IN HISTORY 130

APPENDICES 133

    I. Summer of 1999...................... 133

    II. Summer of 2004..................... 135

    III. The Services Created In The Neighborhood: 1965 - 2004 144

    IV. Significant Events And An Ever-Expanding Local and National Recognition of the F.O.R. As An Effective Neighborhood Development Model 171

    V. The Power Struggle Continues … 186

PREFACE

The organizing work we do in the Sto-Rox Neighborhood is grounded in a belief that life is a gift, and that personal life has real meaning only when lived in service of others.

We believe that each of us is born free, and that freedom in this context leans heavily on the ability to choose to use one's freedom for the good of others. Each time a person decides to live and to act in truth and with integrity, and chooses, in word and deed, to love the neighbor as an other self, he or she begins to know ever more fully the joy and meaning of life. Every such personal choice is a milestone on the journey for each of us, as we make our way on in life, - toward an ever more effective, "whole" and "enwholing" expression of personal freedom in human history.

We believe that life responsibly lived with integrity (mind, body and spirit in harmony within the self, and extended in joyful service to others) is life as it is meant to be. To live in this way requires more than personal effort. It is most effective when it is a collective effort. But it is always both task and gift. It is always life lived as both gracious and graced.

We further believe that creation is an ongoing process and that each self is born to be a participant in the creative process. This belief gives assurance that personal life can be lived with hope. It invites self to be open to each of life's invitations, and, - when invited, - to creatively respond.

But even as any one of us responds positively and generously in the present moment, - difficulties may appear to be overwhelming. Taking responsibility for a crisis or need situation may seem a burden too great for self to bear. But in the proverbial twinkling of an eye, self will soon begin to see the interconnectedness in the whole of reality. Self discovers that he or she is one with all other selves. Self is not alone in the struggle. Given this abiding awareness, the collective self understands and can say, "Yes, together, we can".

Such engaging in the creative process will continue on forever, - even until self experiences his or her final moment in time and space history. For we believe that the original giftor, the unlimited energy source, gives each of us in each moment of time and space, the grace and strength needed to respond.

So it is that in a synchronistic way, we believe that in doing neighborhood development, we commit ourselves, not just to the creation of a health center or a credit union, or a cultural center, but we commit ourselves to the task of awakening hope in each other. Here and now, this experience of working together, - to be servant to and with each other - is somewhat like to, yet unlike, an experience of the unlimited. It can perhaps best be described as the good feeling and warmth, deep inside - that ordinary folks come to know, - when they engage in neighborhood development efforts together.

As organizers, we know well that once the yearning for a better quality of life is stirred into action, it is the inherent consequent of the golden rule that self is thereafter impelled to continue to create, and to provide, meaningful and caring services for others.

This belief is rooted in the historical life of Jesus, who lived in Nazareth, a remote neighborhood of the world two thousand years ago. His historical life is the good news about a free man who lived in love and truth, and who served others to the end of his historical life. Jesus is the free man who defined for us all by his historical life, the freedom to live and to love unconditionally. Jesus is that new and unlimited possibility in history, who addresses every person in history. For each of us, he defines by his historical life what it means to live well. Like Mohammed, Buddha, Elias, Moses, he is an incarnated sign that life has both meaning and purpose; that unconditional love and service of others is possible.

By his historical life, - lived in love, with integrity and in truth, - Jesus gives promise of life forever. By his historical life, he caused a major breakthrough in humanity's understanding of itself. He lived and demonstrated by word and deed the value of one life lived well in human history. He was ever conscious of who he was and who he is forever. He loved so completely and he lived so intensely that every person he met felt loved and lovable, and responded lovingly. It was this response of love that healed and that made whole the sick and the lame and all who came to him.

Jesus did not heal so much as Jesus loved. His love evoked from others a response of love. His unlimited love, his high vibrational presence, made all things whole. The blind saw, and the lame walked and the hungry felt full as he passed by. That life can be so lived, freely and meaningfully by every person, is, in Jesus, a new possibility.

While working in Sto-Rox, we (Father Regis Ryan, Father Donald Fisher, Sister Paulette Honeygosky, vsc) held on to this belief, even as we hewed to the task of living out a decade and more of our personal lives in this particular piece of history. As organizers, part of our task, we knew, was to hold open the horizon of new possibility in Sto-Rox in the fullest possible way. In the areas of education, local government, the development of human services, we attempted to serve as value center, enabler, catalyzer - awakening people's hopes and stirring their wills to choose to organize and take action together, in the co-creative task of the development of their own neighborhood.

Co-creativity is a way, perhaps too long neglected, of emphasizing the incarnational aspect of the gospel. It is joy to create one's reality; it is joy to co-create the piece of the world in which one lives. It was Jesus' joy to do so in Galilee. It has been our joy to do so, together with the people of Sto-Rox, in a Neighborhood, just four miles outside of Pittsburgh, Pennsylvania.

THE TOWN'S INITIAL STRUGGLE FOR FREEDOM: 1969 - 1973

What follows will not be a description in accord with textbook principles of serious social science, but it will give the reader a basic feel for the quality of life, or lack of it, in the Sto-Rox Neighborhood. And hopefully it will also provide an understanding of the open-ended way in which we addressed the challenge of development in this Neighborhood.

When we speak of Sto-Rox, we mean two separate municipalities out of the one hundred twenty-nine in Allegheny County — Stowe Township and McKees Rocks Boro. They are just outside the city of Pittsburgh's southwestern limits, about five miles down the Ohio River from the Golden Triangle or from what is commonly known as the Pittsburgh Point. The two communities are contiguous. Both are equal in population (about 10,500 residents each). They

Paulette G. Honeygosky, vsc

form one Neighborhood, with common transportation routes, shopping facilities, churches, post office and school system. They are old towns; they are working people's towns. Stowe is slightly younger and slightly more residential than McKees Rocks. They are heavily industrial along the river bank and railroad lines, and more residential as you move into the hills away from the river front. The business district is fairly active. Both local business and local government are in deep financial trouble but neither is yet flat on its face. The people of Sto-Rox are mostly white; from a wide variety of Italian, and Eastern European Slavic, German and Polish ethnic origins. The black population is 6% in McKees Rocks and about 1% in Stowe Township. There is a lot of people pride in the Neighborhood. Family structure is disintegrating, but it is doing so more slowly than in most towns in spite of its too many bars and its too few recreational facilities. It is a poor place economically. (Both Stowe and Rox are officially classified among the poorest communities of Allegheny County.) Life is friendly and neighborly in Sto-Rox but enemy lists grow, and suspicion mounts quickly when the topic of conversation turns to politics. There are complicated family and job relationships. The groups whereby people organize themselves — churches, clubs, government, service organizations, —appear to be typically *status quo* but they are deeply entrenched in long-standing allegiances.

In 1965 a simple question was raised and around that question a meeting of the residents was called. The question was: Does McKees Rocks want to begin a human service program under the federally funded Economic Opportunity Act, - a piece of anti-poverty legislation introduced and passed by Congress that year. The meeting was typical enough in that the group wanted the program and knew that the town needed the program. Also, the group was willing to serve and incorporate as a fledgling citizen committee; receive the federal funds involved; and create and administer the program. But this decision and this meeting would have a not-so-typical ending.

The group just formed was almost immediately stymied. Everyone was afraid to approach the McKees Rocks Mayor to ask for his cooperation. But to seek such cooperation (not necessarily permission or authorization) was a procedural requirement in the federal guidelines for the program. In a memo Father Don Fisher wrote:

"When I asked why the fear, the other members of the group at the meeting began to give me a short history course on McKees Rocks. I was told what I was to experience personally, that Mayor David Hershman was not to be approached lightly; that most people stayed out of his way; that meetings of the sort that we were in at the moment were not to take place without his approval, and that we were already in trouble. So, for the moment, the matter was tabled; no

About Ordinary Folks Who Said We Can: & They Did

decisions were taken, but we did agree to meet again to discuss this further."

"When at the second meeting Doctor David Horowitz, a local optometrist, and I (Father Fisher) expressed a willingness to visit the Mayor, we were immediately chosen as leaders of the citizen group. This was the beginning of a whole new movement that would affect many aspects of the public life of the people of Sto-Rox for decades to come.

The Mayor's questions when we went to his office were clear: "Who are you? Who do you represent? What do you want? Who in the hell do you think you are? The final statement of the Mayor, which, of course, ended the meeting, was equally clear and decisive. He said, "I play second fiddle to no one. This meeting is over."

The Mayor of McKees Rocks had ruled the town like a king for over twenty-five years. He controlled countless jobs in the County; in the local school district (which had merged with Stowe Township in 1966), and in the Boro. His patronage job level in the region was well-known. McKees Rocks had more citizens employed in Allegheny County's bureaucracy than any of the other one hundred and twenty-nine municipalities in the County.

County-wide incumbents also knew that the Mayor exercised almost total control of the votes of the residents of the three housing projects in McKees Rocks through his brother, who was for many years, the town's housing manager. The ability of the Mayor to elect or defeat a candidate for public office was legendary. He was, to many who dared not question his power, no further than their latest favor, a benevolent dictator. But to those who felt his wrath, he was a ruthless tyrant.

To be dismissed from his office usually meant just another reason to resent him. To be dismissed on that day in 1965 was different. When the incident was reported back to the citizens' committee, these few people - for the first time in the town's history - decided to fight rather than, once again, let the matter be swept under the rug of political abuse.

"The decision to struggle as a group against the Mayor's closed policies, and his tight autocratic control of everything from the local newspaper to the street cleaner's schedule, was a watershed moment and was, I think, (wrote Father Fisher) the beginning of a new Sto-Rox."

For almost a full year after this decision, there was a battle for power: which faction, the Mayor's or the Citizens' Committee, would receive and administer the anti-poverty federal funds if and when they would come into the town.

During that year there were meetings, conferences, pickets, position papers and leaflets of every description. Well-attended citizen training sessions were offered by the staff.

The Citizen Committee tenaciously held together. They grew in number. And very soon they acquired much fame and notoriety in the region because of the intensity of the struggle, the infamy of the

Paulette G. Honeygosky, vsc

Mayor, and the appetite of the regional news media for good story.

At the end of that year the group was victorious. The Citizens' Action Committee (C.A.C.) was selected to be the legitimate administrative arm of the Anti-Poverty Program in McKees Rocks. Federal funds would come directly to the group without the intervention of the Mayor and the local Boro Government. It was a major victory. The integrity of the program was assured: a federally-funded human service program in the Neighborhood would be administered by neighbors, caring for each other.

Even greater breakthroughs were now beginning to happen in the hearts and minds of many people of the town, both those struggling actively, and those who supported the movement from the sidelines. There was a dramatic surge of empowerment; a new self awareness. **WE CAN DO IT! IT IS POSSIBLE!** For the first time in anyone's memory in this Neighborhood, residents had gathered together to confront Mayor King David. And it would be the first time they would

About Ordinary Folks Who Said We Can: & They Did

stick with many a controversial issue until it was resolved.

Somewhere along the line during that first year of conflict, the members of the citizen group decided to formally stay together for the long haul, as a force for neighborhood improvement and local liberty, no matter the immediate outcome of the Poverty Program conflict.

The citizen group (C.AC.), three dozen persons at most but numerically increasing membership by the day, soon became known as the Citizens' Community Action Committee - **C.C.A.C**. The members now publicly dedicated themselves to the practice of **C**ourage, **C**onviction, **A**ction and **C**ommitment.

At the County level, the group was C.A.C., a non-political entity serving the needs of the poor and elderly in McKees Rocks and Stowe Township. But in the local community, the group, under Jim Garvey's leadership (now Father Jim Garvey, an ordained priest, serving in the Diocese of Pittsburgh) was known as C.C.A.C., a somewhat maverick protest group, calling to task the local power structure.

During the next year of relative calm, C.C.A.C. began to etch out an identity. As C.A.C., it already had a kind of status. It had a small office with staff, a typewriter, and office supplies paid for with federal funds. It was legitimate. It was creating human services for those in need.

But as C.C.A.C., the same group had many political obstacles yet to overcome. It had miles to go.

The most significant advances in the struggle for local liberty occurred rather undramatically as people (more than fifty percent who had not gone beyond grade school) began to learn how to look for the heart of the issue, how to put agendas together, how to conduct house meetings, and how to set priorities, etc. The Citizen Committee sponsored political awareness forums, raised funds with bake sales, initiated adult education classes and created youth recreation programs. In general, the C.C.A.C. took more and more responsibilty for the local turf. One of its most significant cultural and economically rewarding achievements was the annual weekend Nationality Festival, which eventually would attract about forty or fifty thousand people each year to the town. The Festival's success allowed people to speak about their town in a new way. They had created something to crow about.

Much of the controversy concerning the Citizens' Committee and the Poverty Program was centered in McKees Rocks. Stowe was only involved because it was located in the region. This soon changed. Stowe's involvement grew as the new poverty office began to serve the, more often than not, "hidden" needy in Stowe. Stowe's involvement reached new intensity when the C.C.A.C./C.A.C. called the Sto-Rox School Administration (also controlled by the Mayor of McKees Rocks) to task for not including them in the planning of Title I Federally-funded Programs for the educationally challenged.

When confronted by the citizens, the school officials were adamant. The new group was even more adamant.

Paulette G. Honeygosky, vsc

An investigation by the Feds resolved the problem in favor of the citizens. Locally, a new precedent was set for people-participation in public school programming: thereafter, the rule was clear. No public hearings, - no federal funds. Once again, the citizens had won. But very shortly after this victory, there was to be yet another dramatic crisis, maybe a fortuitous one. It was one that clearly evidenced that freedom is not easily won and is not easily sustained.

After a year of successfully administering the Poverty Program, the C.C.A.C./C.A.C. hit a new stone wall. The Greene Amendment was passed by Congress. Congressman Greene, rather than give in to the pressure to completely dismantle nationwide all existing Poverty Programs, proposed a compromise amendment. It was designed to slow down nationally the speed of the programs' demise. Basically the amendment said this: local governments (in McKees Rocks this meant a Boro Council controlled by the Mayor) have the right to determine whether or not the

Poverty Program will continue to exist in their community. Federal funding (in accord with the Greene Amendment) would diminish by fifty percent per year over the next five years, allowing time for local programs to become self-sustaining. Hearing this, and true to form, the Mayor of McKees Rocks had his Council immediately and unanimously vote to end the program. The battle was on again!

For at least six months after that vote of the Council, the struggle raged on full force, but this time the people were organized; they were more astute in planning their strategy, and they were more dedicated than ever to keep intact and to exercise the new liberty they had won.

There was a more skillful use of the news media and there were carefully planned tactics to achieve each of their goals. During this phase of the struggle, there were almost daily sit-ins at the Mayor's office. And the homes of the

Paulette G. Honeygosky, vsc

individual Council persons were picketed daily in an attempt to force a vote change.

Many people later on recounted how difficult it was to stand out in this abrasive way in their own neighborhood for what they believed in. This was different than complaining about the ills of the Federal Government, they said, where the enemy was faceless and far away. In this case, many alliances, friendships, marriages, church committees, inter-relationships of all kinds were put to the test as the battle became the talk of the town.

It was a time of crisis. It was also a time when - in the training sessions for the participants in this new phase of the movement, - the notions of territorial responsibility; of quality of life for all versus power and wealth for a few; of commitment to the long-term struggle, - were hammered out.

It was an exciting thing to see individuals struggle to liberate themselves. Cynics, who had lost interest in politics years before, now began to come on board. It was heartening to see people begin again to take interest

About Ordinary Folks Who Said We Can: & They Did

in their neighborhood; lose their fear; courageously speak up at public meetings, overtly join the movement, and gain increasing confidence in themselves as they began to support even the most controversial of issues.

Local newspapers and TV media came alive in support of the cause of the people. Notably, John Roberts won the Golden Quill Award for his two part TV presentation of the McKees Rocks story.

Somehow in all of this, the camel's back was broken. It is still uncertain which straw did it. The pressure simply became too much. The break came when one of the most unlikely council members, after months of resistance, saw the light and publicly changed his vote in favor of the Poverty Program being refunded and continuing on. One by one the other council members followed suit. A month later, the Boro Council (in the first such action in over twenty-five years on the part of a Council affiliated with Mayor David Hershman) voted to be in charge and stand up to his control over them. It was not long before the Poverty Program

Paulette G. Honeygosky, vsc

was up and humming again. The Council was in the driver's seat and the Mayor, now a silent man at the Council meetings, was a man on his way out.

It was at this point in the struggle that the Catholic Diocese of Pittsburgh funded a proposal for what was to become the F.O.R. (Focus on Renewal) Neighborhood Development Center. In doing so, the Diocese clearly identified with the next phase of Sto-Rox's struggle for freedom.

Much of the citizen movement from that time on would emanate from this new and diocesan-funded Focus on Renewal (F.O.R.) Center, and subsequently, from F.O.R.'s creation, - the F.O.R. Sto-Rox Neighborhood Corporation.

The late Cardinal John Wright came to McKees Rocks for the opening ceremonies and stamped his approval on The McKees Rocks Story when he ecumenically and prophetically said,

"F.O.R. is for all the people of this neighborhood, regardless of race, color,

creed, ethnicity. It is not against anything or anyone."

And he continued, *"We must begin, as the church and in the spirit of the gospel, to see ourselves as elements in a larger whole - the neighborhood, the community, and the nation - all equally beset by crises in education, health, economic self-sufficiency and rising aspirations of ethnic and color minorities seeking their full place in society. We shall implement the role of "church" in the midst of the demands of our times only as we confront these challenges head-on and interact with the total community, with the whole of each neighborhood, to meet them. It is our hope and belief that the F.O.R. Center in the Mckees Rocks and Stowe Township Neighborhood shall truly be, and shall truly do "church", - in the spirit of the gospel."*

HOW THE F.O.R. STO-ROX NEIGHBORHOOD CORPORATION WAS CREATED

In the initial proposal the Diocese of Pittsburgh was asked to fund and staff an open door, ecumenical neighborhood center committed to the development of the Sto-Rox Neighborhood.

Cardinal John Wright officially opened the Focus on Renewal Center on April 20, 1969. At the time it was simply a rented storefront in the center of Chartiers Avenue, the main street of the town. The Diocese of Pittsburgh, with its name clearly visible on the front window, committed itself to the anti-poverty struggle.

The Center was a new reality in town. Its very existence revitalized the citizens' movement. Many wondered how it came about and why Cardinal John Wright himself came to the opening day celebration to give the movement a special blessing. In the light of his visit, the people of the town were a little more inclined to see it as a good thing even though initially most of the local folks, clergy included, gave it little or no support. The Center's credibility was further strengthened by the fact that Father Don Fisher, the Director of F.O.R., was also serving as an assistant at the local Francis de Sales parish.

Because of its new image, its new staff, and because of a respite in the moment from crisis, F.O.R. was able to reach out to the community with more vigor than it had done under any other of its "citizen group" titles in the past.

As F.O.R.'s new Adult Education Coordinator, Sister Paulette, began to conduct small living room meetings in homes on every street of Sto-Rox around people's needs. In retrospect, this phase of the movement was invaluable. It let people know that the pace had been stepped up, and that the much needed human services could and would be made available through sources other than, and even in spite of, the local government.

Paulette G. Honeygosky, vsc

Right from the beginning the message at these living room house meetings was - if we work together, we can outperform the unresponsive local government. *[And eventually, we did.]*

The Youth Program attempted by F.O.R. had a really difficult time getting on its feet. (We had so little to offer to the young people. No parks. No baseball fields. No gyms.) Very early on, the youth effort was discontinued at the discretion of its director, Larry Kessler. *[Years later it would be funded and reorganized, and it would succeed.]*

Quietly the new Center plodded its way through the rather pragmatic tasks of organizing a credit union and a library. The town had neither. Both the credit union and the library owe their initial success to the gentle but firm guidance of a recent widow and housewife, Mrs. Dolores Miller, who in the first years of F.O.R.'s development administered the Sto-Rox Neighborhood Credit Union, and also led the effort to gather library books from everyone's attics and cellars so as to create the town's first library. Dolores had found a meaningful way to serve. Each of the staff or volunteers over the years would likewise do so.

In a letter to a friend, Father Fisher (who knew firsthand the politics of the town) wrote:

"After a year Sister Paulette (who came on board to do Adult Education) and I began working more as a team than at our own pieces of the program. It had not been planned that way but in the first year of F.O.R.'s development, there had been so much reflection, conversation and planning together that the team approach gradually happened. Paulette's reports on her living room coffee groups showed that the Adult Education Program would be far different from the mini-classes in philosophy and theology initially proposed. We now saw that our primary task would be to educate for people empowerment."

Both from among the staff and from among the Center's volunteers, there gradually emerged a common idea and a common commitment: that the Center would be dedicated to really listening to the people and would work toward the development of programs around real and practical needs; that the Center would be a sign of openness and service, no matter how out of the ordinary the witness it gave might appear.

As a result, F.O.R. became increasingly involved in meeting the real needs of real people in this poverty-stricken and overtly politically-corrupt neighborhood. There was no child health care. The town's only doctor had no legitimate credentials: no license to practice medicine. (More often than not, the town pharmacist read the prescriptions, asked the customers about their symptoms, and then re-prescribed an over the counter medicine, that was safer and more on the mark.)

Other human service needs in the town were equally grave. There was no mental health care. There were no nutrition programs in the schools: no breakfast, snacks or lunches for the hungry children in attendance.

About Ordinary Folks Who Said We Can: & They Did

The policies F.O.R. began to put in place were open-ended and designed to effect an immediate, practical response to each issue or need, when and as it surfaced. The F.O.R. Center rather quickly became a place to learn how to be a leader and how to effectively respond to long-standing local corruption and injustice. It became a place to go for coffee and conversation, and a place in which to gather if one wanted to better understand and change the causal factors that were eroding the quality of life in the neighborhood.

With every step forward, the Center's staff had to be more willing to live on the edge. During that first winter, for example, F.O.R. was turned over by the staff, all night, every night, for several months, to the street people; to the young alienated adults of the town. Homeless, they needed a warm place to stay on those cold winter nights. Through this program of "all night warmth and food", F.O.R. achieved a good rapport with the young people, but not a good reputation with the police and the town's "more respectable" folks. Even the town's clergy were upset with the F.O.R. staff over this gesture. [And if truth be told, it was one of the most successful of F.O.R.'s efforts. It was a lesson for us all in what it means to live on the edge and trust. We literally gave the Center to the street people night after night, all winter long.

Motorcyclist, wild-haired Paul Letky would turn up each evening to request the back door key. Some time after midnight, long after staff had gone home for the night, Paul would open the door to the town's homeless. What they did all night in a Center that housed a Senior Citizen Service Program, and a Child Health Center by day will forever be a mystery. But every morning at six, when Father Fisher or I (Sister Paulette) arrived to put the hundred cup coffee maker on, one or other of the "homeless" would be there waiting, to turn back the key, and to say *Thanks*. Most often it was sleepy-eyed, unshaven Rick Hefferman (a former altar boy), who was the last of the night folks to leave. Somewhat sheepishly, he would say, "I stayed to make sure the place was mopped clean, and ready for the day people."]

Initially it had been proposed that the clergy of the town would form the Policy Board of F.O.R. It was hoped F.O.R. would be ecumenically supported and administered by the local clergy. But it soon became evident to Father Joseph Girdis, chosen to organize the Board, that the clergy of the town did not appreciate, much less were they willing to identify with, the early-on confrontational style of F.O.R. So for a while the Policy Board of F.O.R. existed in name only. The staff took its policy cues directly from the people.

Over time, however, there was a real need to develop an administrative structure for the F.O.R. Center. If F.O.R. was to truly belong to the people, its *modus operandi* would have to change. A Citizen Board, not the staff, needed to take center stage, and the board members would need to be elected from the natural leaders that every neighborhood has.

A decision was made to incorporate as a tax exempt, non-profit corporation; write by-laws; elect a Citizen Board, and begin to function as a legal entity.

New questions now surfaced. How could the staff make all that the F.O.R. Center is, was and would be, belong to the people? How could the staff assure that everyone in Sto-Rox felt invited to belong? For whom did F.O.R. speak? Did F.O.R. have any right to speak for anyone?

Corporate structure alone would not resolve this dilemma. F.O.R. could only speak for people to the extent that a way could be found that would allow the people to speak for themselves. Every person living in the neighborhood needed to be invited to be a member of F.O.R. : that was a part of the answer. It was clear that the F.O.R. staff needed to again visit every home in the neighborhood to get this message to the people.

Another part of the answer was that block meetings needed to be organized,

About Ordinary Folks Who Said We Can: & They Did

and residents on every street needed to identify and learn to speak in behalf of their own turf needs. Only then could people really take responsibility for the street on which they lived.

As we prepared to launch this second all-out, comprehensive organizing effort, we searched for new insights. We talked with old friends; with experienced organizers from across the states. We contacted and consulted with new ones. As often happens, the search for the way to proceed opened the way to the next stage in the development process.

At first the question of how to approach our new organizing task included a plan to wait for foundation monies and additional staff. For weeks we waited. But finally the decision was made to go forward with volunteers and whatever resources we could muster on our own. To invite and maximize the participation of the people of the neighborhood in F.O.R.'s decision-making process: this was our new goal. Come to the F.O.R. block meetings was our new mantra. Creating enthusiasm for this notion was like pulling teeth at times, but it was a solidly grounded conviction, that once come alive, would not die.

By day we walked the streets. At night we did the paper work. The F.O.R. Corporation by-laws began to take shape. With the generous *pro bono* help of a profoundly insightful lawyer friend, Lou Loughren, a skeletal model for the new Corporation charter was drawn up. Then at regular town meetings, for nine consecutive months, the people assembled and they worked out the details of a document that they could approve and live by. Article by article was discussed; a vote on each article was taken; a decision was made. Night after night, we repeated the grueling process. Finally, dressed in its new legal by-law clothes, F.O.R. was ready to meet the public as the F.O.R. Sto-Rox Neighborhood Corporation. We strutted with pride through every street in Sto-Rox and made our way to every doorstep with our new message.

"We have discovered a way to take back our neighborhood," we said in living room

About Ordinary Folks Who Said We Can: & They Did

after living room in Sto-Rox, every night of the week for a whole summer."

Our house visits and nightly meetings were reinforced by follow-up phone calls and leaflets. Five thousand phone calls per month; five thousand leaflets per month, five thousand home visits, and sixty neighborhood meetings in three months time, - it was an arduous task. For the most part, that summer we went underground. "Where is that group which had been so active?", some folks asked. The local paper carried the time and place of our meetings, but the announcement was a strange word to the town. Block Seventeen will meet tonight. Block Twenty-one will meet tomorrow night. That was it. Nothing more. Nothing very dramatic.

The long summer of organizing twenty-one Block units (during the summer of '72) was over. We were tired! But we were exhilarated. We had laid the foundation of a genuine grassroots organization. The

Paulette G. Honeygosky, vsc

people had become the F.O.R. Sto-Rox Neighborhood Corporation!

About Ordinary Folks Who Said We Can: & They Did

FAITH-BASED REFLECTION

We believe one of the highest manifestations that a person is free is the ability to choose : to either acccept or to refuse an option presented. Positive responses are possible. Refusals must also be possible. Each choice, - negative or positive - in turn, evokes the many other options that have not yet surfaced.

So even as we recognize that negativity is real, we know that its power to kill the freedom movement is illusory for a refusal is itself an expression of freedom.

Allowing is the life stance that sees both the negative and the positive as warp and woof of every moment of historical life. Both are necesssary to the success of the process of being and becoming that a vibrant, developing neighborhood will experience.

PROBLEM SOLVING IN THE NEIGHBORHOOD

It was now time to put the intense organizing effort that preceded this moment to the test. We describe below two problem solving situations in which we engaged. The first is the Health Center story. It illustrates F.O.R.'s successful planning strategy to accomplish an objective, - even when the citizens were confronted by the inertia and longtime neglect of irresponsible public officials.

The second is the Ambulance Story. It describes F.O.R.'s less successful attempt to enable the citizens to cut through very direct and heavy-handed opposition from the town's elected officials.

THE HEALTH CENTER STORY

Almost from the day the F.O.R. Center opened in 1969, the staff recognized that health care for the children was the town's major need.

So in early September of 1970, the staff began discussions with the designated regional providers of health care in general, and pediatric care in particular. F.O.R. staff arranged meeting after meeting to which the administrators of Ohio Valley Hospital, Allegheny County Health Department, Allegheny General Hospital and the Regional Hospital Planning Association were invited. By February, 1971, at about the fifth or sixth meeting of this working coalition of health care providers, a proposal for possible pediatric care at an independent McKees Rocks site, under the sponsorship of a citizen group, was presented to them. At the time, neither the funding nor an organized Health Council existed. But good faith abounded. The need was self-evident. Wonderful things began to happen.

Once the idea of a Neighborhood Health Center was in principle accepted by the health-providers, the F.O.R. staff lost no time in convening a Sto-Rox community town meeting with parents to talk about pediatric health care. This meeting took place in January, 1971. Over one hundred citizens attended even though the night was wintry cold and it was snowing heavily. On this night, from the ranks of the natural leaders in this assembly of concerned parents, the Sto-Rox Child Health Council was formed. The group was apprised of the general health-related contacts with the appropriate State, Federal and Foundation potential funders that the F.O.R. staff had already made. They were also informed of the results of the many meetings that had been held with the region's health care providers. Before that first citizen meeting ended, the group had chosen their executive officers; set up a schedule of monthly meetings, and

About Ordinary Folks Who Said We Can: & They Did

prepared a prioritized list of things to do. The need was that urgent!

Very shortly after its formation, this embryonic Health Council had an opportunity to raise money with the help of the Bonaventure University Band and Choir, who at their own expense travelled to McKees Rocks from Olean, New York. Two concerts were held. Before each concert the Health Council volunteers prepared and served supper to the performers. They sold concert tickets and generally organized and hosted the event. When the last note was played and the second concert ended, the Health Council had raised a net profit of $750.00 for the Health Center. (This was an appreciable sum to raise in a poverty neighborhood where the residents could little afford the luxury of spending monies to attend a concert. But they did. The cause was right. The town's goal was one step closer to reality. Bonaventure University had given Sto-Rox much more than music on this concert night.)

By March 1971, the Health Council had created its own research commmittee

Paulette G. Honeygosky, vsc

whose job was to develop proposals and seek state, federal and/or foundation funding for the proposed Child Health Care Center.

Also at this time an anonymous gift of $4,999.99 was received by the Health Council. It was accompanied by the group's pledge to send $100.00 more each month during the first year of the Health Center's operation. This very heartenng springtime gift and pledge, which followed so closely on the heels of the Bonaventure University fund-raising concerts, made the Health Center seem even more of a possibility. Thereafter, the Health Council's efforts became increasingly more specific; more pragmatic; more determined.

A meeting between the residents and the regional health providers was arranged. It was very effective. Doctors and appropriate Regional Agency Administrators heard firsthand the stories parents told about the unmet health care needs of their children. Mothers wept. Fathers argued. Why won't you please help us : this was the poignant question

About Ordinary Folks Who Said We Can: & They Did

parents asked the providers, eyeball to eyeball.

Not surprisingly, several important decisions were made during this meeting. A site was chosen.

It was decided by the Health Council and the regional health providers that the future Child Health Care Center for the Neighborhood would be set up in the basement of the F.O.R. Center. (The original storefront F.O.R. at 610 Chartiers Avenue had an unused basement, which the carpenters and electricians of the town agreed to renovate and which the women promised to furnish.)

It was also agreed that the professional service staff of doctors and nurses would be provided by Allegheny General Hospital. Ohio Valley Hospital agreed to provide ancillary and emergency room back-up, and also offered the services of their accounting department. [This gesture on the part of Ohio Valley Hospital was an absolute necessity in the beginning in order for the Health Center to immediately be able to process the patients' Medicaid and Disability forms.

Paulette G. Honeygosky, vsc

F.O.R. did not yet have its provider State certification number. That would come a year or more down the road.] And the Allegheny County Health Department agreed to provide, at no cost to the Center or patient, the inoculation serums and supplies needed for the children's long overdue immunizations.

Even so, at this point, when all was said and done, the proposed Child Health Care Center was nothing but a storage basement in the F.O.R. storefront office. But the parents were undaunted. The day after the meeting with the providers, a few very determined members of the soon-to-be-incorporated Health Council began to visit local merchants to request the donation of building supplies, carpets and medical equipment. Beginning with six or seven doors for the examiniing rooms, obtained from a local lumber company, the Health Council and its volunteers systematically obtained the donation of every pipe, screw or nail - of everything

About Ordinary Folks Who Said We Can: & They Did

- that was required to renovate the basement.

Skilled workmen of the town began, the very next night after that very decisive town meeting, to actually work on the renovation of the basement. All through the month of September, 1971, the neighborhood's carpenters, electricians, plumbers, painters and carpet layers volunteered (after their regular day's work) to create the Sto-Rox Neighborhood Child Health Care Center in the basement of the F.O.R. Center. (While husbands and fathers worked through the night in the basement of the F.O.R. Center, mothers and grandmothers kept the coffee pot on the first floor going. They also made sure the refrigerator was stacked with hearty sandwiches.) When finished, the estimated total value of the Child Health Center (labor and materials) was over $10,000, - of which less than a few hundred dollars had actually been spent.

The Health Center was completed just the night before its grand opening, the celebration of which took place on

Paulette G. Honeygosky, vsc

October 1, 1971. A clinical session for the first sick child, Bernard McNally, occurred five days later on October 6, 1971.

And by November 14, 1973, the Sto-Rox Neighborhood Child Health Center recorded the medical history and care of its 902nd child patient, Eric Voye. This number would reach a million and more visits over the next three decades, a record of service to the children of Sto-Rox in which the Sto-Rox Health Council (now incorporated) and the F.O.R. staff, then and now, takes great pride.

It was part of F.O.R. staff's organizational model that the Health Council Inc. would take group membership in the Sto-Rox Neighborhood Corporation. [From the very beginning, F.O.R. Sto-Rox Neighborhood Corporation saw itself as the umbrella corporation for the incorporated service units it would create over the next several decades. Over time, this model would prove to be very effective: weaker corporate units were supported by the stronger. Well-funded corporate units inter-loaned and helped to keep other service programs afloat when their funding was cut and/or their existence was threatened. It was a very functional and very effective organizational policy.]

In July of 1973, the Sto-Rox Health Council Inc. was sufficiently organized and ready for group membership in F.O.R. Sto-Rox Neighborhood Corporation. So, together with the F.O.R. Sto-Rox Neighborhood Corporation, the Sto-Rox Health Council Corporation, committed itself to the Sto-Rox Neighborhood. Both corporations agreed to take responsibility, not only for expanding the neighborhood services they each rendered, but they also agreed to work closely together to improve the quality of life for the residents of Sto-Rox.

The Child Health Care Center (opened in '71), the Staunton Clinic McKees Rocks Counselling Center (in '72), the Dental Care Room (in '74), the Neighborhod Family Blood Bank (in '74), and the Senior Citizen Health Management Program (in '74) : all of these health care units were incrementally developed. They were organizational steps on the way

Paulette G. Honeygosky, vsc

toward a free-standing medical facility and a comprehensive family health care program, that at this stage was but a dream, but a decade later, would be and is in 2004, - a reality. A real success story, then and now.

THE AMBULANCE STORY

"In October ('72), members of the F.O.R. Neighborhood Corporation made an effort to develop an ambulance service for Sto-Rox that would not only transport patients to the hospital, but would provide emergency care from the moment contact was made with the victim. There is much that can be said about life-saving assistance to the patient in the time before the ambulance reaches the hospital. Proper care can prevent further injury to the victim. Ultimately, proper care can save a life. There are many instances of harm that can happen when an injured person is approached by someone who does not know how to help the injured person properly because they know little or nothing at all about emergency medical care.

But trying to get someone in this town to say "Yes, that's important. Let's do something about our ambulance service," and then getting them to act is a painfully

Paulette G. Honeygosky, vsc

slow process," wrote neighborhood resident, Nurse Welsh.

In October of 1972, F.O.R. began to canvass every home in Sto-Rox to see if the residents would support a subscription-type plan for improved ambulance service. (Each resident would pay a minimum annually; federal funds would take care of the rest.) Fully equipped vehicles and trained personnel, for which federal funds were available, would have been part of that plan.

But very soon, true to form, the local police, were, in typical backroom decision-making style, "ordered" by the elected officials to block the door-to-door canvassing. On the first day of the drive, - F.O.R.'s subscription-plan advocate, Pat McMahon, was arrested in the home of a resident, who lived next door to Councilwoman Loretta McCabe. No excuse; no rhyme or reason given for the arrest. She was simply handcuffed, taken to the police station, and within minutes was released. But the word of this arrest put the fear in F.O.R.'s other subscription-

About Ordinary Folks Who Said We Can: & They Did

plan advocates. In addition to the threat of arrests (a scare tactic on the part of the elected officials), the "politically-controlled" regional newspaper did its best to confuse the issue in Sto-Rox even though it did an excellent job of promoting such an ambulance service plan in the neighboring town of Ingram where what it wrote was noticeably less biased.

Because not enough of the townspeople could be given the facts (door to door canvassing was blocked by the threat of arrests; the newspaper would not publish the facts), the subscription plan was abandoned. A new way had to be found.

The next step was a protest visit by the residents to the Stowe Township Commissioners' meeting. One resident after another complained at the meeting about the inability of the police and firemen to perform lifesaving measures in Stowe's stationwagon ambulance. At this meeting the Chairman of the Commission agreed that he and the Township's Safety Commissioner would meet with the F.O.R staff to discuss the ambulance improvement plan. With the help of Gary Burnsworth, Director of the Valley Ambulance Authority, such a meeting was held. Mr. Burnsworth explained that if federal funds were to be invested in an ambulance service, it could only happen if two or three towns worked together to create a joint ambulance service. He explained that the goal of the federal authorities was for Western Pennsylvania to one day have a well-coordinated Western Regional Ambulance System.

With hopes stirred, F.O.R.'s ambulance meetings with residents were held almost every month in some part of Sto-Rox. To one such neighborhood block meeting, all of the Rox Councilpersons and all of the Stowe and Kennedy Commissioners were invited. Not all of the elected officials attended. But Ted Talkowski from neighboring Kennedy Township did, and he let it be known that the township did not want to be involved in the plan. Ted said that the people of Kennedy were satisfied with their present ambulance service. (This was not so. Very much like the situation in McKees Rocks and

About Ordinary Folks Who Said We Can: & They Did

in Stowe, Kennedy's ambulance service consisted of a stationwagon vehicle with no emergency care offered to the patient on the way to the hospital. Like Stowe and McKees Rocks, Kennedy, too, has had more than its fair share of emergency room DOA's (Dead On Arrivals).)

After Kennedy Township's withdrawal from the planning sessions, a proposal was written only for Stowe and Rox. It outlined a service that the residents could trust and respect. The proposal was signed by Mr. Joseph Cusano (Stowe) and Mr. Bob Taylor (McKees Rocks) with the consensus of the Stowe Commissioners, and the vote of a majority of the Council Members of McKees Rocks.

But even as the proposal was being signed by these elected officials, McKees Rox firemen and some of the nay-saying members of the McKees Rocks Council, silent heretofore, began to make their opposition to the plan heard. Fireman Al Logue, writing in the *McKees Rocks Gazette*, clarified the firemen's opposition. He said that the firemen's objections stemmed from their fear that volunteers would move in on them and eventually take over their jobs.

He claimed, too, that "Our union doesn't allow us to work with volunteers."

(But the fact of the matter was that the Rox paid-firemen, when fighting fires, regularly worked with the volunteer firemen of Stowe. That argument was moot.)

Nonetheless, the obstacles were clear. The paid-firemen of Rox did not want to work with Stowe's volunteer firemen, nor did they want further training. They offered excuse after excuse as to why they could not attend the life-saving training classes that the local Ohio Valley Hospital agreed to sponsor.

Taking patients to any of the hospitals within a ten mile radius was not possible either, they said, because, during the time required to do so, not enough firemen would be left on duty at the station. Nor would they agree to allow a non-fireman, an Emergency Medically trained driver, to use the ambulance to take someone with a crushed skull, for example, to Mercy Hospital where head injuries are best treated, or to the cardiac unit at Saint Francis Hospital where the patient's doctor was on staff. No matter the condition of a particular patient, all patients were simply delivered to the Ohio Valley Hospital Emergency room.

This talk about unions and about working with volunteers was just another way of acting out regress. But it was something of the last straw. It brought the months of effort to improve ambulance service in the neighborhood to an abrupt halt. Politically it was both untimely and inopportune to press the issue further.

F.O.R.'s public statement at the time said it all. To the readers of our statement we said:

"We had a proposal for improved ambulance service in Sto-Rox. It was signed, funded and waiting to be implemented. 50% of the cost of fully-equipped vehicles for Stowe and Rox was to be covered by a federal grant. There would have been radio communication

between vehicles, and between dispatching centers and receiving hospitals. Eighty-four hours of no cost paramedic training was available for all ambulance service personnel in Stowe and Rox.

> *But it's over.
> Rox firemen have won.
> The town's sick and dying have lost."*

Even after releasing this "what might have been" public statement, we made one final effort in McKees Rocks. (It was just so hard to quit.)

We scheduled a meeting to which all the elected officials of McKees Rocks were invited. But now that the firemen had objected as they did, none of the Rox Council members, who initially had supported the proposal, even bothered to attend this final meeting. Nor was any Rox Council member, who was actually present, willing to say a positive word about the proposal. At this final meeting the proposal was simply rejected. A vote was taken to retain the present

About Ordinary Folks Who Said We Can: & They Did

ambulance service in McKees Rocks (a delivery system to Ohio Valley Hospital, with no emergency medical care on the way).

By this formal action of the McKees Rocks Boro Council, the proposed funding for Stowe Township's improved ambulance service was also lost since the federal money had to be used for improvement in both towns, or none.

"We can all rest easy, I guess, with the decision of Phil Schiralli, Loretta McCabe, Joe Adamcik, Regis Berner and Elmer Pello, all of whom were present and silent at that final meeting, and with the decision of Bob Taylor, Edward McNabb, George Babin, Stanley Roman, who chose to be absent from the final meeting. The Rox Council, without a word of reasonable explanation, voted to retain the ambulance service McKees Rocks now has.

We can rest easy with their decision as long as none of us or none of our loved ones are in any serious accidents or ever

Paulette G. Honeygosky, vsc

suffer a cardiac arrest." So wrote nurse Dolores Welsh, a resident of Stowe, who led and lost F.O.R'.s struggle for improved ambulance service for the Sto-Rox neighborhood.

But notwithstanding all this effort and apparent failure, F.O.R. had lifted the town to a new level of awareness of what was lacking in their current ambulance service. Now the town really wanted an improved ambulance service.

Understandably then, a politically-supported, profit-making entrepreneur moved into the vacuum and developed a pay-as-you-go ambulance service that he knew the consumers would now be willing to pay for. When all is said and done, this privately-owned ambulance service was an improvement over the service formerly provided by the Township and Boro elected officials. Unfortunately, it was and is an additional expense that most folks in the Neighborhood can ill afford. But it's there. And they use it.

About Ordinary Folks Who Said We Can: & They Did

FAITH-BASED REFLECTION

We reverence and live life in freedom, but we do so with regard for, and not at the expense of, the freedom of the other.

Neighborhood problem-solving is to be done in such a way that neither self, nor neighbor (other self) is ever reduced purely to someone for whom something is done.

Rather, we are to create services and programs together, - for each other.

When the urgency to live life in freedom conflicts with an other's inertia or opposition, the Word about freedom again needs to be heard. An announcement needs to be made for all to hear: that tension caused by inertia or opposition can be addressed, embraced, lived with, and sometimes, it can once again be transformed into renewed energy for creative change.

THE TOWN'S GROWING PAINS
May, '72 - March, '73

(As described by Katherine D. Gordon, Pitt University Graduate Student)

In September, 1972, Katherine D. Gordon, graduate student at Pitt University, Pittsburgh, asked to do her field placement work in the neighborhood of McKees Rocks and Stowe. James Cunningham, University Faculty, served as Field Supervisor. Kathy's Field Placement Evaluation is printed below in part:

"The philosophy of F.O.R.", she wrote," places strong emphasis on process development. The objectives are to encourage the citizens to grow in freedom, and to structure a new system of governance in which the citizens have a voice, and through which the citizens will begin to assume responsibility for the well being of their own community.

The approach to community organization that F.O.R. uses is to encourage and foster block by block group dynamics as a force for community participation. This organization model includes visiting every residence and developing one-on-one contacts on each block, - all the while laying the groundwork for block meetings of neighbors with their neighbors.

This effort is also designed to identify the natural leaders on each block, and encourage them to convene block meetings where neighbors could discuss their needs, set forth their goals, and pragmatically spell out ways to achieve results when any decisions were taken."

For a period of two months the Pitt University Graduate student fully participated in this evolving organizational process and attended each of the pre-designated twenty-one, block by block neighborhood meetings. The student worked with each block chairperson to plan and organize the block meetings,

Paulette G. Honeygosky, vsc

facilitated the process at the meetings, and monitored the follow-up on the decisions made and the actions to be taken. The student then described her experience in each of the twenty-one organizational block units.

Block One. This unit is a County Housing Project, namely, the Ohio View Acres. A power struggle, a kind of "turf battle" precipitated an early-on split between the F.O.R. staff and the existing Tenants' Council. The conflict led the County to refuse F.O.R. permission to use the Boys Club, the only available meeting place in the housing project. Kathy's recommendation to the natural leader who emerged: continue making one-on-one contacts within the neighborhood unit. And when timely, reorganize the F.O.R. organizational block unit around the existing Tenant Council. Following the election of new officers, let the Council wear two hats: let it be both the Tenant Council, and the F.O.R. block group. This strategy worked, thanks to the leadership of one of the Housing Project residents, Marge DiPerna. (The F.O.R. Membership was eighty-one persons in this block assembly in September of 1974. But by 1974, a new problem had surfaced: there were too many leaders; too few followers.) *[Nonetheless, a clear task was gradually identified and a decade later, the citizens' efforts led to the construction of a Senior Citizen High Rise in Neighborhood Block One.]*

Neighborhood Block Two. This Italian-settled and highly politicized neighborhood, locally referred to as Norwood, began with a reluctant leader (s), namely, a husband and wife team, Bill and Charlene Vales. The feeling of the majority of residents on this block was one of clear opposition to the against-the-local-politicians' movement, which to many, in the beginning, was what F.O.R. represented. (Many of the elected Stowe Township officials lived in this neighborhood and so this attitude was to be expected.) But it was believed that if a task was defined that would offer benefits to all, it would then compel the block neighborhood's support. (The F.O.R membership was only eight persons in September of 1974.) There was for most of that first year, no strong leader. And no compelling task was identified. Somewhat inane tasks were proposed. They were: that several rat-ridden and abandoned homes on the block be razed, so that a neighborhood park could be created.

[Surprisingly, a decade later, - both tasks were accomplished in Neighborhood Block Two. Also, several public officials who lived in this neighborhood were reported by empowered residents, their "neighbors", to the tax authorities. Several of these elected officials were subsequently imprisoned for fraud and embezzlement of tax monies.]

Neighborhood Block Three. This unit, known locally as the somewhat isolated, below the bridge, Preston neighborhood, began as a group with strong leadership. The group succeeded in getting the Stowe Township to repair a major street on their block by staging

About Ordinary Folks Who Said We Can: & They Did

a street blockade. But after this initial success, the group experienced a very real setback. It fell apart when its chairperson resigned. She chose instead to devote fulltime to a more safe and a-political F.O.R. service; she agreed to help develop what was, as yet, the very embryonic Neighborhood Food Van Co-op. (The leader of this unit had bowed to the political pressure of an elected official, who was her neighbor, and who controlled her husband's job.)

Clearly the leader's allegiance to F.O.R. was weakened. She was torn within by concern for her husband's job and her genuine yearning to be of service. This conflict eventually caused her to completely break with F.O.R. Kathy recommended that the F.O.R. staff try to pull together all the factions in this neighborhood by focusing attention on a common task, that would benefit both friend and enemy on the block. (Membership was twenty persons in September of 1974. Also, there were too many leaders; too many factions in the group.)

[But a common task was eventually identified: the group agreed to work to bring about the repair of the foot-bridge, - a much used shortcut across the river to the town center. A decade later the foot-bridge in Neighborhood Block Three was finally repaired.]

Neighborhood Block Four. This residential unit had a leader with a real commitment to the task of creating a new traffic pattern through their section of town. Numerically large, the group provided considerable support to their chairperson, Harry Mackey. The neighborhood defined its problem - the truck traffic that went up and down their street. The group was working well together to have the traffic re-routed. Good follow-through. (But actual membership was only twenty-four persons in September of 1974.) *[A new traffic pattern on Singer Avenue was eventually established. The heavy truck* *traffic thru this residential area was re-routed.]*

Neighborhood Block Five. This is a block neighborhood with no defined leadership, and little or no committed membership. The student observer recommended continued outreach to find a leader and identify a task that would pull the group together. Eventually a natural leader, Phyllis Seibert, was identified and a task was agreed upon: to do a door-to-door Senior Citizen Need Survey, which would be focused on the needs of the many elderly living in this Stowe Township block area. (Membership was thirty-nine persons in September, '74.)

[This survey was completed and several months later, based largely on this invaluable collected data, a comprehensive senior citizen service proposal was written. When funded, a comprehensive senior citizen service

program was begun in 1974, under the able direction of Rick Welsh.]

Neighborhood Block Six. A leader has emerged, and is personally canvassing the neighborhood, door-to-door. The leader's support group is growing. The task has been defined: to publish a citizen-owned newspaper, and to organize an ecology-focused clean-up. These decisions were made at the meetings, but the group's follow-through was weak. (Membership was thirty-six persons in September of 1974.)

[Eventually the clean-up and the removal of large areas of poison ivy growth was done. And less than a year later, the first issue of the F.O.R. newspaper was published. It survived for several years and contributed much to F.O.R.'s organizational success. Over the years, the need to publish a newspaper again surfaced. This time it was only published for a year or more. But the need for a newspaper has gradually been

eliminated. An informative F.O.R. website has replaced it.]

Neighborhood Block Eleven. A small steering group meets each month on this block. Several members are already personally involved in F.O.R.'s service programs in the Neighborhood. But there is a reluctance on the part of any of the residents on this block to publicly take leadership responsibility, or to clearly define the neighborhood's priority task. The group has no leader. But individuals on the block did agree to do a Senior Citizen Need Survey in McKees Rocks. (Membership was thirty-six persons in September of 1974.)

[The data from Stowe's survey that was done by residents of Block Five, when combined with the data in Block Eleven's survey in McKees Rocks, clearly documented grave and unmet senior citizen human service needs in both the Rox Boro and the Stowe Township. The housing data from the combined surveys led eventually to the creation of the Sto-Rox Plaza Housing Corporation, and the

Paulette G. Honeygosky, vsc

building of a Senior Citizen residence in McKees Rocks. Based also on this comprehensive housing need data, an unused, former convent building was converted into a halfway house for the emotionally and physically challenged.]

Neighborhood Block Twelve. This area has a strong leader with a very committed following. (The membership was forty-two persons in September of 1974. A leader has emerged.) Tasks defined: to develop a neighborhood park, and to request that traffic lights and safe crossing lanes be put in place on Chartiers Avenue, which is also Route 51, a state highway that runs through the center of town. *[It took years of lobbying at both the County and the State level, but both of these objectives have actually been achieved.]*

Neighborhood Block Thirteen. This area is a housing project with its own Tenant Council. The Council became the F.O.R. organizing group and was content to wear both hats, thanks to the leadership of Ida Bryant, Audrey

Gross and Loretta Farrell. (Membership was twenty-four persons in September of 1974.) Task: to develop a children's educational program in the meeting room in the Housing Project.

[The "L" Children's Program was created. It provided a learning and enrichment experience for the children living in this housing project. It was the seed that eventually grew into a day care facility in the center of town for the pre-school children of the Sto-Rox Neighborhood. It also brought to light the grave need in the Neighborhood for the Positive Parenting programs, eventually developed by and through the F.O.R. staff's efforts.]

Neighborhood Blocks Fourteen & Fifteen. This was a strong active group that pursued two very vital issues: post-Flood Agnes Urban Renewal, and the removal of several oil storage tanks located dangerously near to a residential area. Block Fourteen merged with Block

Fifteen to form a strong pressure group ready and able to resolve these issues.

(Membership was one hundred and five persons in September of 1974. Sandy Wolf, a natural leader did emerge.) Defined Task: to monitor the federally-funded Redevelopment Plan for this flood-prone region.

[Over time and after a lot of conflict, the citizen's voice prevailed. Flood Gates were built. New housing and first time recreation sites in the area were developed. The traffic pattern was changed. And the Pitt Oil Company's storage tanks were moved away from the residential area.]

Neighborhood Block Eighteen. This area has a dedicated leader, Dolores Welsh, who has a profound appreciation of the objectives of the F.O.R. Neighborhood Corporation. But in her own block unit, the leader's support is weak. Many of the local politicians live on her street and give her a hard time. (Membership was only eight in September of 1974.) Defined Task: To develop a neighborhood playground. *[A playground was never developed in this area, - but when a new grade school was built, the school play area served well as a neighborhood playground. Meantime - way back then, this group became heavily involved in improving the town's ambulance service. Although the federally-funded ambulance service plan was voted down by the elected officials, the Sto-Rox ambulance service was improved when the Boro and Township service was replaced by a privately-owned, for-profit business.]*

Neighborhood Block Nineteen. This area has a reluctant leader in a very politicized block neighborhood. But the leader has real commitment, and does seem to understand the goals of the F.O.R. Neighborhood Corporation. This neighborhood unit is middle class *status quo*. The group has few members. Perhaps a clearly defined task could one day pull the neighborhood together. (Membership was twenty-five in September of 1974.)

A task was defined: To repair pot holes and to plant trees in this neighborhood. *[These tasks proved too inane to serve as a reason for this neighborhood unit to really get involved. There were a few symbolic responses, but they were often individual, not group responses. For example, one or two residents purchased the materials needed and actually filled-in the potholes on the street on which they lived.]*

Neighborhood Block Twenty-one. This neighborhood unit began with an active group that immediately defined several tasks. But less than a month later, the chairperson resigned because he was hired to be the Boro solicitor.

Clearly, leadership and membership support in this block was always uncertain. (The situation was like the fox guarding the hen house. Many of the elected officials, whose policies F.O.R. opposed, lived in this section of town and they attended the block meetings just to hear what F.O.R. was up to.)

(Membership was fourteen in September of 1974. All leaders. No followers.)

Their selected task: to offset industrial pollution. *[Planning this project was largely academic. It was a joke! There was no industry in the town, - much less was there industry operating among these million dollar residences. For the most part these meetings were simply a welcome diversion for the wealthy, - for the politicians and the professionals - living the good life in this part of town. This neighborhood's only contribution to the good of the whole was the lesson it taught us about human fallibility.]*

The Board of Directors. "At the end of the first year of the block by block organizing effort", Kathy Gordon wrote, "the chairpersons of the twenty-one territorial block units were invited to become the Board of Directors of

Paulette G. Honeygosky, vsc

the F.O.R. Sto-Rox Neighborhood Corporation".

It is clear, concluded Pitt University student Kathy Gordon, that F.O.R.'s commitment to process development is both its strength and its weakness.

Its commitment to the development and growth of personal freedom and responsibility through active grassroots participation forces the organization to reach for higher ground, - to reach for a genuine transformation in human behavior. (By contrast, an advocate organizer needs only to consider how to accomplish the goal advocated. For example, opposition to a new school - for the advocate organizer - requires action that will simply stop a non-needed new school from being built.

But the process-committed organizer, which F.O.R. is, needs to consider not only how the building and tax burden of an unwanted school can be opposed, but must also consider the practical consequences to the community, to the children, and to each person involved in the protest.)

An organizer committed to the ideal cannot ignore the reality of where people engaged in the process are in their personal self-growth. Too often organizers stress only tangible and measurable accomplishments. What happens to the folks engaged in the process doesn't seem to matter.

But it does concern F.O.R. Caring about folks is both F.O.R.'s weakness and its strength.

Can task advocacy be separated from people development? To set goals and then ignore the consequences in the lives of the persons involved in accomplishing them has too often over the years contributed to the demise of far too many neighborhood development groups.
But where the issues are clear, - when active participation is encouraged, and a balance between process and advocacy is maintained, - good things happen. Both

Paulette G. Honeygosky, vsc

personal satisfaction and healthy self-esteem grow with each accomplishment.

"F.O.R.'s staff", wrote Kathy Gordon, "seems to care too much, rather than too little, about the folks involved with them".

About Ordinary Folks Who Said We Can: & They Did

FAITH-BASED REFLECTION

To proceed into pragmatic neighborhood development action from open-ended faith convictions, requires that we, carefullly and often, engage in reflection upon the people development process that is also unfolding before us.

To do so is to engage in problem-solving and organization-building in such a way as to offer people the widest possible range of options through which, perhaps timidly at first, and then boldly, express their personal freedom as they create new realities in their neighborhood.

This is an arduous and never-ending process. But we believe that mustard seeds planted today will flourish many times over tomorrow.

PEOPLE OF STO-ROX EVER MORE IN CHARGE

The following excerpts are from the actual minutes of the Community Assembly (s), Town Meetings, from April 1973 through July 1974. If you read these minutes, as you would read a caseworker's record of a decade or more of evaluations of a client, these minutes will clearly demonstrate the Neighborhood Corporation's growth and development as it became an increasingly more healthy and effective corporate self.

Corporate Selfness. The numerical increase of F.O.R.'s membership was astounding. F.O.R. had thirty-two members in May of 1972, - as compared with three hundred and thirty members in March of 1973, and seven hundred and eight members in September of 1974. As the membership grew, the programs and services multiplied. The reverse was equally true.

Corporate deliberate and responsive growth. Determined and studied decision-making together was well underway. Grassroots folks, not staff, were now in charge of the Corporation's programs and services. The issues voted upon at the town meetings were increasingly complex and demanded responsible follow-through. The Town Meeting Assembly, not the staff, now held the new block leaders and Program Directors accountable to each other.

First Community Town Assembly, March 5, 1973. At this first town meeting, held in the Presbyterian Church hall, the motion to be voted upon was: that the Keverline Building be purchased for no more than $24,000.00, and that the Board of Directors be empowered by the Assembly to complete the negotiations and make the purchase without delay. After a great deal of debate, the motion was put to a vote, and it was passed.

Second Community Town Assembly, June 20 1973. The first motion for discussion and vote at this town meeting was the administration model for the F.O.R. Sto-Rox Neighborhood Corporation. The motion read: When a program or service (for example, a health center, senior citizen center, credit union) shall be developed by the F.O.R. Sto-Rox Neighborhood Corporation, the following shall be adhered to:

The President or Chairperson of each Program or Service shall serve *ex officio* as a member of the Executive Board of Directors of the Neighborhood Corporation.

All funding for F.O.R.'s programs shall be initially received by the umbrella-like F.O.R. Sto-Rox Neighborhood Corporation, but these funds may then be held in separate accounts and administered by the Director and Board of the specific Program for which the funds were designated. The Community Assembly shall approve the hiring of the Directors of the various Programs, but the Board of each Program will interview and recommend their choice of a Program Director. Each Program Director is directly accountable to the Board of Directors of the Program, and each Program

About Ordinary Folks Who Said We Can: & They Did

Board of Directors is, through their president, directly accountable to the Executive Board of Directors and to the General Assembly of the Neighborhood Corporation. The motion was discussed, voted upon, and approved.

The next motion at this town meeting concerned the remodelling of the Keverline Building, initially purchased as an investment. *[Eventually it housed the office of the Senior Citizen Service Program, administered by Rick Welsh. When that program was relocated to the F.O.R.-owned building at 701 Chartiers, and when F.O.R. lost its federal funds, the building was sold as a way to keep the F.O.R.'s human service programs afloat.]* The proposal was favorably received, but it was amended before the final vote was taken. The amendment required the Corporation Board to advertise the specs, to receive at least three bids, to award the best and lowest of the bids, and to supervise the remodellling.

Paulette G. Honeygosky, vsc

A third motion at this town meeting dealt with the relocation and expansion of the Credit Union. The plan was to move the Credit Union from its location in a rather obcure corner in the F.O.R. Center to a front street location. (More specifically, the suggeston was to move it into the old CCAC office on upper Chartiers Avenue, - to an office so tiny, it had once been used as a janitor's supply room, - but it was on the front street and that was important). The plan also was to hire two part-time workers at a hundred and twenty dollars per month for one year. One part-time worker would take care of the books, and receive deposits and payments. The other would be an outreach worker in the community and take responsibility for securing new members and collecting delinquent loans.

The rent at the tiny office was $15.00 per month. Utilities were extra. Salaries plus rent and utilities would amount to approximately $3,000 per year.

The Board of Directors of the Credit Union would include a person from each block neighborhood unit. Each of its various committees would be similarly constituted. The President of the Credit Union Board would be *ex officio* a member of the Corporation's Board of Directors.

The Credit Union Committee had at their Executive meeting discussed this plan, and they asked at this town meeting for the Community Assembly's vote and approval. The motion was voted and approved.

The fourth issue voted upon was the "Anywhere in Town Bus" proposal [the embryonic beginnings of the ACCESS transportation system, eventually developed by F.O.R.] . The "Anywhere in Town Bus service", as proposed, would begin with a volunteer who would drive the van four times a day around the town, making seventeen stops on each trip around. No fares would be charged, but donations would be accepted. This motion passed but was qualified. The service was to operate only for a trial period, after which the program would be evaluated. If it proved to be successful, a full-time driver would be hired. The Assembly voted to spend a hundred dollars to finance the experiment.

The fifth motion was a proposal to publish a newspaper to inform the Sto-Rox Community about what is really happening in the town. The local newspaper, controlled by the political machine, was a constant source of anti-F.O.R. news reporting.

Voted and approved: that the Corporation sponsor its own newspaper; that the Staff and Board research the best way to do this; that the Corporation publish the newspaper on a trial basis for two months; and that a report on this newspaper experiment will then be brought before the Community Assembly for evaluation. When the motion passed, Richard Scrabis volunteered to be the first newspaper editor.

Issue six concerned the Health Center Reorganization Proposal. A motion was voted and approved that the Health Council Board include one member from each of the twenty-one neighborhood block units. Its President would be an *ex officio* member of the umbrella F.O.R. Sto-Rox Neighborhood Corporation Board of Directors. In that way, although the Sto-Rox Neighborhood Health Center is a legal entity in its own right, the F.O.R. Sto-Rox Neighborhood Corporation is co-responsible for the Health Center.

Third Community Town Assembly, July 11, 1973. Issue one was that of Home Rule. A position paper on Home Rule was distributed to the Assembly; it was then read aloud. Line by line the paper was discussed. Questions were asked and answered. What is Home Rule? What could Home Rule mean for McKees Rocks and Stowe Township? After lengthy debate, the following motion was approved by the vote of the Assembly: that the Corporation support the effort to put the Home Rule Question on the November ballot; and that the Corporation put on the same ballot a slate of seven persons, who supported local government by town

Paulette G. Honeygosky, vsc

meetings, as candidates for the proposed Home Rule Study Commission.

Issue two was a motion requesting assembly support of a proposal to formally protest building a new high school. A Position Paper describing why there was a need to oppose the construction of a new High School for Sto-Rox - to be built not in the neighborhood of Sto-Rox but in Kennedy Township - was then read. It suggested that the Sto-Rox High School remain at its present location. It agreed that improvements on the old high school be made, but it also put the Sto-Rox School Board on notice that a new school, on a site four miles outside the town, would be opposed every step of the way. (The homeowners in Sto-Rox were already paying the highest school taxes in the County, even though census data indicates that as a neighborhood, Sto-Rox is so median-income poor, it qualifies for anti-poverty federal funding.) A motion was entertained that the Assembly endorse the Position Paper as read. By unanimous vote, it did.

A new motion - issue three - was then made: that the Corporation initiate protest action to enforce the Position Paper by picketing the homes of the individual School Board members. And if that failed, then, as a last resort, it was proposed that a picket line form at the building site and an attempt to stop the bulldozers be made. This motion also passed.

Fourth Community Town Assembly, November 14, 1973.
No voting took place at this assembly. Due to a severe snowstorm, a voting quorum of a hundred persons was not present.

Fifth Community Town Assembly, February 6, 1974.
A motion was made to send a letter of protest to the Boro Council. The letter was to stipulate that the Council violated the United States Constitution when it did not permit Father Fisher and Sister

Paulette G. Honeygosky, vsc

Paulette to speak at the Boro Budget meeting, (especially since at that same meeting, the Council allowed two other non-residents to speak). Legal steps for relief are being taken.

Sixth Community Town Assembly, March 6,1974.

Voting issue one: Public Service Employment Contracts. After considerable discussion, it was agreed by unanimous vote that the Neighborhood Corporation work with the State and continue to create Public Service Employment (PSE) jobs for persons on assistance who are seeking employment.

Voting issue two:
Use of the Methodist Church Building. By vote of a previous Assembly, it had been agreed that the Corporation contract for the full and unqualified, leased use of the Methodist Church building.

But when the contract was drafted by the Church Council, it contained a clause stating that the church could be used only for Senior Citizen programs, and no other Corporation programs. Since full and unrestricted use of the building was the key issue in the original negotiations, a motion was made to renegotiate the contract. The new contract should allow for full and unrestricted use of the building for two years, and should stipulate that utilities, insurance and maintenance costs would be paid by the Corporation. If the contract could not be written with these allowances, - after thirty days, negotiations were to cease and a search for another building should get underway.

Voting issue three: The McKees Rocks Bottoms Redevelopment Project.

It was agreed that the Corporation submit a letter of intent and make the required good faith deposit of five thousand dollars to purchase property for a basefield field in the Redevelopment Area. Since the good faith deposit would be returned if the purchase of property for a baseball field was not consistent with the overall Flood Redevelopment Plan for the area, the motion was unanimously passed. The purpose of

Paulette G. Honeygosky, vsc

this application was to give voice and vote to the Corporation in the Flood Redevelopment Planning, now underway, since only property owners were eligible to participate directly in the planning process.

Seventh Community Town Assembly, May 9, 1974. A motion to request the Corporation's lawyer and friend, Lou Loughren, to investigate the possibility of a suit against the School Board was voted and approved. The issue was the building of the new high school at a four mile distance out of town without Public Hearings, and without regard for the increased tax hardship the homeowners would incur.

Eighth Community Town Assembly, July 24, 1974. Voting issue one: whether or not to create a community-based credit union. Would such an institution more adequately meet the credit needs of the residents? Would it not provide the entry of thousands of people into the mainstream of financial services?

About Ordinary Folks Who Said We Can: & They Did

(A community-owned credit union could allow many of the poor and homeless to open an account and take out a loan to buy a car, to send a child to college, to bury a family member, etc. Most banks consider persons on welfare too great a credit risk. But a community-owned credit union could take that risk.). The motion was put to a vote and approved.

The motion also authorized the staff to seek out credit union experts like Father Geno Baroni for advice on how to secure capital investments in the credit union. (Baroni advised that we first ask the more affluent in the neighborhood and in the nearby suburbs to become substantial, no-interest depositors in the credit union. These deposits would then become the start-up capital loaned to, and then repaid by the needy.) More than two decades later, the credit union has a net worth of a million plus, and is primarily used to send the town's young people to college. The

Paulette G. Honeygosky, vsc

loan payback rate is more than ninety percent.

Voting issue two: the Senior Citizen Service Assurance Proposal. When the County cut the funds for the Center's Senior Citizen Service Program, the matter was taken to the Town Assembly. The Assembly voted in the Assurance Plan. For a $1.00 per week, per year, the Senior Citizens of Sto-Rox would be assured of the services formerly offered under the County federally-funded program. These included, then and now, transportation, home repairs, financial counseling, nutrition education, health care and information/referral services.

Both issues were discussed at length, voted upon, and were passed.

About Ordinary Folks Who Said We Can: & They Did

FAITH-BASED REFLECTION

Life with meaning is essentially life that is heart-centered and profoundly faith-filled. It is ordinary life transformed.

This belief proceeds from a conviction that creation has already happened, and yet creation continues to happen. Whether or not we will it to be, each day's new reality happens. It invites us to embrace it.

The Zen Buddhists have an expression that addresses this: "The sun will rise. The grass will grow itself.".

THE TOWN'S NATURAL LEADERS TAKE OVER, AS THE HOME RULE QUESTION SURFACES

By May of 1974 the F.O.R. staff had become more like consultants to the natural leaders who emerged as a result of the many facets of the neighborhood's struggle for self-governance.

When, for example, the Corporation took on both the Township and the Boro in the long battle for a citizen voice in spending the newly-legislated Federal Revenue Sharing monies, that was to come into the Neighborhood, - the town folks, without much direction from the staff, were ready and equal to the challenge.

Now when the elected officials raised the old question: Who are you and whom do you represent?, very ordinary citizens responded, "We are the Sto-Rox Neighborhood Corporation, which holds regular public meetings in every part of this community and to which everyone is invited. We represent the people. Whom do you represent with your closed doors and backroom politics?"

The resentment of the elected officials increased with each such citizen challenge. Members of the corporation were repeatedly denied entrance to the public meetings. Many times the Corporation members were physically forced by the police to leave the public buildings. Citizens' attempts to develop a process for the spending of the Shared Revenue monies were blocked. The local newspaper controlled by the elected public officials harshly criticized the "maverick" Corporation members. The staff of the Corporation, even when silent at the meetings were harassed, and at the slightest provocation, staffers were arrested. But these arrests and this harsh treatment backfired. The Corporation members became bolder with each instance of such treatment. They pressed for voice and vote on the issues.

Down the road their efforts would yield success. But in the weeks ahead, the

Paulette G. Honeygosky, vsc

going was tough. A little victory here; a little victory there. But for the most part, the elected officials held sway. No matter. People empowerment was well underway. More boldly by the day, the people struggled to create a new quality of life for each other.

Like most other community organizations, the F.O.R. Sto-Rox Neighborhood Corporation spent much of its time, talent and energy in the endless search for funding. F.O.R.'s annual Diocesan funding only provided money for rent, utilities, basic supplies, crisis intervention and limited program development. But in no way did it cover the costs of the various programs and services that the Neighborhood Corporation offered. And there was no money for staff salaries. Volunteerism reached an all-time high in Sto-Rox.

Gradually the Health Program, the Credit Union and the Senior Citizen Association began to take more responsibility for becoming self-sustaining units of the Neighborhood Corporation. Each entity in turn wrote proposals and aggressively sought its own funding; over time, each succeeded in being funded and in becoming self-sustaining.

But as this was occurring, a new idea surfaced. Questions were now raised concerning the Mayor and the Boro Council's irresponsible use of power. If we, the citizens of Sto-Rox, are delivering so many neighborhood services, isn't that governing in a sense? Do we not have a right to these services and shouldn't they be paid for with tax monies? In fact, shouldn't we, together with our neighbors, have a greater share in the governing process above and beyond just choosing a candidate for office at election time. We were now treading deep water! But we had support. That year Senator Mark Hatfield of Oregon came to McKees Rocks and talked about people taking charge of their neighborhood. His visit and his speech gave us new hope. Several months later Senator Hatfield introduced into Congress his Neighborhood Self-Government legislation. He cited McKees Rocks in the

Paulette G. Honeygosky, vsc

Congressional Record as a model of what self-governance can achieve.

The notion of self-governance gradually became clearer. Sto-Rox Neighborhood belonged to the citizens. Yet it was being governed by elected officials who no longer represented the citizens who elected them. Citizens had given the elected officials their power, but the officials in turn continually abused it! It was time to take it back! The question would no longer be - which representative shall we elect, but rather, do we need to have any representatives? The search for answers slowly uncovered a new way to proceed into the future. The question was not whether or not to take back power. Rather, the question now became - when and how best to take it back.

Act 62 provided the key. Act 62 enacted by the Pennsylvania State Legislature gave to a local community (like Stowe Township and McKees Rocks) the right to elect a Home Rule Study Commission. This Study Commission, once voted into office could not only study the structure of their local government,

About Ordinary Folks Who Said We Can: & They Did

but could actually prescind from the Boro and Township Codes written by the State Legislature, and could then draft and present to local voters a new charter for governance, more appropriately suited to their own neighborhood.

It was an Act that afforded the voters an opportune moment to move toward self-government by and through town meetings. Against the wishes of the elected officials, the Neighborhood Corporation gathered the needed signatures and put the question of Home Rule on the ballots in both the Boro of McKees Rocks and the Township of Stowe. Shall McKees Rocks (shall Stowe Township) elect a Home Rule Study Commission?

The Corporation won that part of the battle. The answer of the people to the referendum on the ballot on the next election day was Yes. And two Study Commissions were elected: one in McKees Rocks and one in Stowe Township. But the Corporation was not successful in achieving that which was the most inventive in the process. Only two of the Corporation's slate of seven candidates for the Home Rule Study Commissions in both Stowe and McKees Rocks were elected. The Corporation's candidates for the Commission were committed to local government by town hall meetings. No Mayor. No political machinery. Government by Town Meetings, with an Executive (somewhat akin to a C.E.O.) who would implement the decisions made at the Town Meetings. A dramatic platform, but, admittedly, still only a minority view.

GIVE THE GOVERNMENT BACK TO THE PEOPLE was the slogan seen everywhere in town. It was the message carried by the local postal clerks, who delivered the circulars from the F.O.R. Sto-Rox Corporation to the five thousand homes in the neighborhood.

The basic message on these circulars was older than the Constitution itself. "If you elect us (the F.O.R. slate of seven Home Rule Study Commission members) to the Home Rule Study Commission, we will give the power to govern back to the people assembled at Town Meetings. The elected officials, under the new charter we will write, shall do the legislative will of the assembled neighbors, who in their town meetings will make the best decisions they can for the good of each other."

The Corporation fought the good fight but it had now hit an impasse. It was in a minority position on the Home Rule Study Commissions in both McKees Rocks and Stowe. The next nine months were filled with brain-storming sessions on how to impact the Study Commissions with only a minority voice. Although the Corporation's effort was directed to keeping the notion of assembly power uppermost in the minds of the Home Rule Study Commissioners and the residents of both Stowe and Rox, it soon became clear to the F.O.R. staff that more dramatic steps were needed if assembly power was ever to become a reality in the town.

The F.O.R. Corporation now began to question the fairness and ineffectiveness of the majority/minority representative system of government. It questioned the representative

Paulette G. Honeygosky, vsc

value of the Commissioners who were elected to the Home Rule Study Commissions. F.O.R. even began to question the representative value of its own candidates who were serving as the Corporation's representatives on the Home Rule Study Commissions. F.O.R. went so far as to say that none of the elected Commissioners represented the people who voted them into office. (The majority members would not; the minority members could not.) Very soon therefore, the Corporation's Town Assembly began to act like a Home Rule Study Commission. Even as the minority Corporation Commissioners continued to attend the official Home Rule meetings, and tried their level best to impact the Study Commissions, the Corporation's Town Assembly met and discussed and wrote new charters for the Stowe and Rox neighborhoods.

In McKees Rocks, opposition to the notion of Home Rule was fierce and quite public. In the beginning, the Rox Home Rule Commissioners did not show up at their regularly scheduled meetings.

About Ordinary Folks Who Said We Can: & They Did

They tried to keep the time and place of their meetings "secret". They held meetings in each other's homes. Finally, when they could no longer withstand the persistent public clamor for citizen input, they convened closed executive sessions in the Boro building's backroom. When the citizens demanded to be admitted to these executive meetings, they were policed out of the Boro Building on two different occasions on two consecutive weeks. But then the media and State officials, when alerted by F.O.R., took action, - and in the third week, the Home Rule Study Commission meetings were held in the regular Boro meeting room, and they were once again open to the public at large.

"The place to change things is at the ballot box" is the usual by-word of the representative system. But the control of the vote in local elections where not to vote, or to vote for other than the machine's nominee, means job loss and carefully orchestrated arrests, parking tickets, evictions, building code permits denied or revoked, buildings condemned, etc, - does not allow for free and fair elections.

So near the end of the long Home Rule conflict in Sto-Rox, the F.O.R. Neighborhood Corporation decided to make full use of the power which Act 62 conveyed. The Corporation decided to go to the citizens with a door-to-door survey and ask their opinion about the effectiveness of the Home Rule Study Commissioners representing them. Were they satisfied with the efforts for change being made by the seven representatives on each of the Commissions?

It was hoped that these survey results would give the Corporation's minority representatives on each of the Commissions a basic tool with which to impact the Home Rule Study Commissions' reports soon to be officially filed and published.

A survey form was accordingly sent to every registered voter in Stowe and in McKees Rocks. Even though only about 20% of the registered voters in each town actually responded to the survey, the results were significant. In McKees Rocks where the registered voters numbered 5,455, - 1,176 people voted YES to the notion that all major decisions of local governments should be made by the people assembled at town meetings. Only forty persons voted to retain the present system in McKees Rocks of "backroom" decision making.

In Stowe Township where there were 6,279 registered voters, 1,156 persons voted in favor of the Town Assembly form of government. Only seventy persons voted to keep the present system

When these survey results were made public, the "controlled" Home Rule Study Commissions in both towns became more determined than ever to exclude from their reports, anything that would hint at returning power to the people assembled at a town meeting. The charter drafted by the politically controlled Stowe Home Rule Study Commission simply rubber-stamped the same charter under which Stowe had operated for decades. Same - o; same - o. No change.

In McKees Rocks the charter drafted by the equally controlled Home Rule

Paulette G. Honeygosky, vsc

Study Commission was simply the old and tired representative system dressed in new clothes. The few suggested changes were merely cosmetic.

The town folks read with dismay the proposed charters, which were to be placed on the ballot at the next general election. The question that surfaced at the F.O.R. Corporation's town meeting, prior to the upcoming vote of the electorate, was: shall we settle for a slight improvement on the old system and get what we can? Or, shall we continue to press for deeper reform even though it might be years in coming?

The voters' answers were heard long before their NO vote was cast at the ballot box. At a Neighborhood Corporation Town Assembly, citizen after citizen raised their objections to the newly proposed Stowe and Rox Charters. The Corporation's minority Commissioners read their prepared "official" minority report to the Town Assembly. It essentially rejected both charters because "they give no voice or power to the people other than to allow them to vote once a year on election day". A few weeks later, on election day, the town voted NO to the Home Rule Charters on the ballot, that were written by the controlled Home Rule Study Commission's majority members.

The people assembled, now wiser and more determined than ever, decided to, once again, put the referendum on the ballot in the next election, and again in the next election. Each time they did so, they understood a little more clearly that they needed to vote YES on the referendum question, and that they also needed to elect seven out of seven Home Rule Study Commissioners who would write new Charters that would GIVE VOICE AND POWER BACK TO THE PEOPLE EVERY DAY OF THE YEAR. It was a commendable empowerment effort. It has created over the years very well educated voters, but it didn't ever fully succeed. The power of the elected officials over people's lives was and is that entrenched. So time and again, the people voted in the machine-supported candidates. They knew that if they didn't, it was a question of having or not having a job; of having

Paulette G. Honeygosky, vsc

or not having a place to live; of being or not being free from subtle threats and harassment. F.O.R.'s proposed Home Rule Government by Town Meetings - that was placed three consecutive elections on the ballot - was what they wanted, but they thought they had to settle for local government, the way it was, in order to survive. *... Nonetheless, the seed has been planted.*

FAITH-BASED REFLECTION

When staff lets go and moves on, it is not to be construed as a sign of failure, disdain, fatigue or discouragement.

To the contrary, "letting go" on the part of staff is a positive sign of authentic leadership. It is leadership that recognizes and affirms that a neighborhood "has arrived" at an appreciable stage of self-development and is able, from that time on, to make it on their own.

AN OPEN-ENDED DEVELOPMENT PROCESS: 1974 - 2004

It's almost thirty-five years (from April, 1969 to 2004) since F.O.R. (Focus on Renewal) was created. An updated word needs to be spoken. Many of F.O.R.'s goals are not yet achieved. But many have been realized.

That F.O.R. continues to serve as an enabler, organizer, catalyzer and value center can be seen in the Appendices' of this book, that offer a rather comprehensive listing of: 1) the new services created in the Neighborhood from 1974 to 2004; 2) the significant events in the life of F.O.R., and the ever-expanding local and national recognition of the F.O.R. as an effective Neighborhood Development Model, and 3) the ongoing and ever present "againstness" and politically-motivated efforts to forever silence F.O.R.'s cry for justice for the poor, for the homebound aged, for the exploited, for the disadvantaged.

Having experienced and reflected upon these realities, I marvel at F.O.R.'s membership growth. (In 1974, F.O.R. already had 2300 members. At the time of this writing in 2004, it can safely be said that F.O.R. is the town. All the town folks are invited to its meetings; all the town folks participate at one time or another in its programs; all the town folks come for one service or the other. It is that comprehensive in its achievements over three decades.)

I marvel also at the racial, cultural and ecumenical diversity of its people support base. Town meetings have been held regularly and, unlike that first meeting when it was difficult to assemble even ten persons in a meeting room, a required voting quorum of one hundred persons is now present, no matter the weather or the issues.

I also marvel at the local people's increased financial and moral support of the F.O.R. Center, that was once described as the radical center to be avoided. It is now referred to as "our F.O.R", which has done so much good for the town.

And I marvel at the Stowe and Rox elected officials, who for years were insensitive and indifferent to the human service needs of the people of the town, but who are now legislating for health care, parks, senior citizen services and improved ambulance service. It may not be for the right reason, but many of the elected officials are now actually competing with F.O.R. to serve the needy of the neighborhood. They, too, have learned. (But notwithstanding, both now, and perhaps much more in the future, F.O.R. continues to outperform the Boro and Township Governments.)

One can only hope that F.O.R.'s voice for justice will continue to be heard; that caring people of the neighborhood will one day accept public office as an invitation to truly work for, and with, the people of the neighborhood they are elected to serve.

Home Rule and governance by and for the people is slowly becoming a reality in

About Ordinary Folks Who Said We Can: & They Did

McKees Rocks and Stowe, not by vote, but by the back door. Now the people's slogan on their protest placards might well read: WE HAVE BECOME THE GOVERNMENT BY OUT-PERFORMING THE GOVERNMENT.

PEOPLE GREW TALL IN THE STRUGGLE

Nowhere in the world are there people with the genuineness of the people of Sto-Rox. People in Sto-Rox are either genuinely good - or genuinely less than good (in the politically not free sense). There is very little pretense. This will become more clear as we describe them in this account of how we remember our experience among them.

It is good to describe them from memory in that memory broadens the perception of goodness, and softens the perception of less than goodness. But somehow, the whole picture from a distance is seen in perspective and all is good.

In the beginning of our organizing effort among them, the people were distant, sometimes hostile toward us. Even safe adult education living room discussions on *"How to Cope with Teenagers"* were written

About Ordinary Folks Who Said We Can: & They Did

off. Few attended these sessions. It was clear that that wasn't the way to proceed.

But what was? During the first year we searched to find a common ground. Afternoons and evenings, daily, we tirelessly invited the residents to coffee hours, changing the content and the style at every turn. But it was clear from the word go that the use of such *"listening to the teacher"* sessions was not the way.

Gradually, two ways (actually one) surfaced. When we would listen to the residents one on one about their human service needs, and about ways to challenge the political structure that exploited and tax-burdened them, there was more than a spark of interest. Our decision to educate and empower them around their own bread and butter issues was merely felt in the beginning. But it soon became clear to both the residents themselves and to us, as the year went by, that this was the way. People grew tall in this dialogic process. They began to look us straight in the eyes and say, "I think."

Somehow we had conveyed to them that we really did want to know what they were thinking and feeling, and did want to know what they needed in their homes and for their families, and in the neighborhood in which they lived.

Over that first year of visiting every home in the neighborhood, we experienced the full range of responses. Some folks wanted things to change, but pulled back in fear when the empowerment struggle began in earnest. Others joined in the struggle, but then returned to the "enemy ranks" where the favors were. Some waited on the periphery and watched for years before entering the strugggle. Some wives came to the meetings without their husbands or families knowing they were there. Some husbands came without their wives or families knowing they were there. Some came, drew back, turned away, and then allied with F.O.R.'s critics and betrayed their initial response. Some never came, but they also refused to join with

About Ordinary Folks Who Said We Can: & They Did

those, who wished to block the F.O.R. neighborhood development process.

But in retrospect, and even in the moment of its happening, it was all o.k. Light and darkness, - ups and downs - it's all part of the dynamic of human development; of neighborhood development. And all of it is good. Reality is one.

For each setback, each moment of darkness, is but another step into the moment of light that follows. And the new light is brighter for the darkness that preceded it. Both darkness and light are experienced on the way to freedom. They are complementary. Every today holds forth hope for a new tomorrow. It is the way. Ignorance is transformed as each new decision is taken and each new understanding is awakened.

But what did it look like, then and now, this people development? Yes, it has names and it has faces, and it has tears and it has laughter. It has concerns and it has joys. It's all there in every minute, in every day, in every shape and form.

There is Ella Oliver. We affectionately called her Bishop Ella because of her royal Hungarian bearing and her elegant style of dress. She loved jewelry and always, - her silver gray hair piled high on her head, was crowned with a diamond-studded hair comb. And from her neck, a pendant sparkled. It was her style of dress, - morning, afternoon and evening.

Ella's love was deep. She believed in F.O.R., without knowing fully what it was that we were attempting to do. She didn't understand much of our fancy words, but she seemed to read our hearts. She followed us in picket lines and protest meetings in faith. For Ella, God had sent us to help her and her neighbors, and that was enough. She was ready to follow, no matter the risk. Like so many others, she simply decided to have us as her leaders.

In the beginning of the movement she walked with us in laughter and with strength. She enjoyed the excitement of each moment. But over the decades of struggle, her steps got slower and more painful as her advancing years and arthritis took hold. First she walked the picket line with a cane. The pain was there. Then she had to resort to a wheelchair. Even then, however, she rolled on with us in the picket lines. Towards the end, as the years added up, there were only her phone messages of encouragement and our occasional visits with her. Through it all, she continued to say, "Keep going. I love you. I believe in you. No matter what the others say, you can always count on me." Even at the time of this writing, an invalid and almost totally confined to her bed, Ella believes and still sends us her message, "You must go on. Don't stop. I believe in you." (d. October, 1989)

It's strange, but the next person that comes to mind in this people overview is Joe Hruska, the town alcoholic. Every town has one, but every town doesn't have one with a history like Joe's. Many a cold winter morning Joe would be found by the police lying on the river bank half-frozen in the snow. After spending a few days in the hospital, Joe would

Paulette G. Honeygosky, vsc

be back on the streets. One day he actually stumbled into the creek and when found was near death from drowning. He survived. Then came the day when he was hit by a passing motorist. He survived. Mal-nutritioned, anemic and suffering with bone cancer, he survived. His survival rate was astounding.

But when he was moreorless sober, in-between his heavy drinking bouts, he would drop into the Center for coffee and conversation. He was a most likable fellow and quite astute. He played the strange role of a friendly critic. He liked F.O.R. He approved what we were about but he didn't think it would work. He evaluated F.O.R. against what his friends the local police were about. He alternately swore at the police, and then he swore at us for being so politically dumb. He thought we were too naïve, too gentle. You have got to play it rough, he advised, else the politicians will beat you down.

At least with Joe our gentleness paid off. He sobered up, got a job, rented a furnished apartment, and came into some money by way of insurance claims over

About Ordinary Folks Who Said We Can: & They Did

an accident settlement. Joe made it - for a while. Or maybe this time, it's forever. With Joe it's hard to predict. (Joe recently died but he willed the remainder of his insurance monies to the F.O.R. Center as he said, "to keep the coffee pot going and help others like you did me.")

There were interesting family patterns for getting involved with the F.O.R. Center. Sometimes, as with Kate McGowan, the wife came on board first. The husband (deterred by a postal worker job situation) never really came into the movement. His job was at risk and so he remained in the background, but we knew that, like so many others in somewhat the same situation, we could count on him.

For many families this was the way it was. The fear of losing their jobs kept them silent and aloof, but they knew that what the F.O.R. Center stood for was just and right.

Kate's unique talent was her gift of rhythm and rhyme. She put to music, and to words, many an issue. And so it was that standing in the picket or protest line, in wind and snow and rain, we would sing our way to victory. We were always ready for a musical celebration of a moment of justice achieved. WE SHALL OVERCOME and DAISY, DAISY were our best known and most used melodies.

To the tune of Daisy, Daisy, we sang:

School Board, School Board Give us your answer true. We're half crazy For the high taxes we give you.
We can't buy food or houses, We can't buy shoes or blouses, So now we say, we shall not pay, Your new tax on us today.

That sort of rhyme in many a moment lifted our tired bodies and our weakening spirits. And we went on, bolder and taller, - and each time we did so, - we sang more loudly than the time before.

Another family pattern was that of Al Spataro, who came into the movement alone. His wife was too sick to come with him. That was the way it was in the beginning. But five years later, when inadequate storm sewers caused twelve inches of back-up water and raw sewage to flow into the more affluent homes of the

About Ordinary Folks Who Said We Can: & They Did

residents on Holmes street, his wife came into the movement. Each new issue drew those, who were, directly affected into the struggle. This new energy was always most welcome.

Together, with Al's wife and the folks who lived on Holmes street, we faced the problem of how to bring pressure to bear upon an incompetent local government that failed to maintain its storm sewers. What little else do we get in return for our taxes? Such was the cry heard from young and old who lived in the flooded four hundred homes. It was like the straw that broke the camel's back. It was the issue that affected many of the moderately wealthy who, for years, unquestioningly had paid taxes levied by an incompetent and corrupt political body. Now, about to experience heavy damage to their homes, living as they did with the threat of every storm backing-up into their cellars, they began to address and protest the government's years of incompetence and dis-service to them. Al's wife and her neighbors, at long last, came to the F.O.R. Center, and actually led the F.O.R.-

sponsored tax revolt. What's interesting is that by this time, Al was too crippled with the effects of a recent stroke to do other than encourage his wife. He could no longer join actively with her in the protest.

There were other patterns. Entire families joined in the F.O.R. struggle. Parents and children grew up and grew together in the movement. Mary Koger and Fran Hogan were blood sisters, and they both brought their families to F.O.R. where as a family they served, and as a family, they grew in age, wisdom, grace and joy.

Friday nights were a special human growing moment for the families involved with us. It was a celebrating moment. We prayed and laughed and sang and cried and encouraged and joy'd and had coffee and special desserts together. By the end of the evening, both the Moms and Dads and the children were folding five thousand newspapers, preparing for the monthly fund-raising Roast Beef Dinners, trimming the Christmas tree, making the endless posters, or planning a neighborhood picnic. The families were there. And it was a beautiful sight to see Moms and Dads and the children working and celebrating together.

For these families, the Center was their second home. The Roast Beef Dinners, the proceeds of which were used expressly to expand the Health Center, were theirs. The shut-ins were theirs. F.O.R.'s concerns were theirs. F.O.R.'s tasks were theirs. They generously lifted the burden from our shoulders onto theirs. And they did so, even though their family of seven or six or five already asked so much of them. We learned early-on that the busiest persons in town were the most generous and the most willing to do more.

Ed Hogan, a nuclear plant supervisor, was special. His faith-filled gesture of taking the specially prepared Roast Beef Dinners to about ten of the most recluse and eccentric of the town's shut-ins is commendable. He and the youngest of his children, Meighan, climbed the stairs, up and down, to the attics and basements where the shut-ins were to be found. Having visited with them and delivered

Paulette G. Honeygosky, vsc

the dinners, he then went home to care for their foster infant child, so that Fran, his wife and his seven other children, could serve dinner to the walk-in elderly of the town, for whom the home cooked dinner, served in graceful and grand style at the F.O.R. Center, was looked upon as very special. A grand Sunday place to go and a real treat!

And there was Frank Koger, another Dad, whom we remember as the person who could make anything broken work again. While the rest of us had coffee and conversation on a Friday night, he would first check this and that around the Center. Then he would join us momentarily for coffee, only to disappear. We would later discover that he had put up a shelf, put in a couple more wall plugs, fixed a leaking pipe,- whatever. Always he served with so much quiet unassuming love.

To say that Frank served with so much quiet, unassuming love brings to mind Sue Riser. She seemed to be always available. One learned quickly to depend on her; to count on her, no matter

About Ordinary Folks Who Said We Can: & They Did

the task, no matter the weather. She is a French-born woman who married a U.S. military man, now deceased. She clearly understood the work of the F.O.R. Center to be the living message of the gospel. Doing the gospel with others for each other, - that's what she was about. And that's what she is all about still. As needed, as called, she responds. More, she anticipates the need and seems always to be the receiver of the gift, rather than the giftor, - that she is. She shops for the shut-ins. She makes soup at the Center for the eighty or more who drop in daily at lunchtime. She knows that they drop in because it's a place where loneliness and hunger and poverty and pain are quickly forgotten in the warmth of the atmosphere, and the heartiness of the lunchtime homemade soup. She's so much a part of that warmth.

    Sue also finds time to stamp the outgoing mail and to do the extras. She speaks hope to everyone she meets

Paulette G. Honeygosky, vsc

as she walks her dog through the neighborhood.

Her command of English is admirable. More than any of the other volunteers, she often writes and has had her *Letters to the Editor* published on issues of local, national and international concern.

Of young adults like Carol Riser, Donna Miller, Mary Ellen Moran, Sharon Wolf, Dave DiSantos, Glen Cybator, Bernard McNally, Robert Sutey and Chester Bridickas, - so much could be said. Each is coping with their own career and life directions, yet each finds time to give a little service to others more needy than they in the neighborhood.

There are so many others to remember. But, as described above, such is the quality of the people of the Sto-Rox Neighborhood. They are people, who stand tall. They are our people. They are our hope as we move together into the Future.

And then there were the …

F.O.R. STAFF DOCTORS VISITING WITH THE ELDERLY HOMEBOUND IN THE NEIGHBORHOOD

"Hello, Louise. We're here with the doctor to visit with you." That's the way an afternoon with the homebound begins for Father Ryan, Doctor Landen or Doctor Bender, and Sister Paulette. "We have entered the apartment of an elderly woman, age seventy-six, who is in the painful last stages of bone cancer. Sometimes we find her alone and lying precariously at the edge of her bed. With no caretaker, she is too weak to roll to a safer spot. So we lift her up and over into a more comfortable and much safer position on the bed. When the doctor's exam and care is completed, we return from the kitchen where we have been waiting to chat a moment with Louise. "Don't forget me. Please don't ever forget me" is voiced in her eyes and is louder than her pain or her need for medicine.

Paulette G. Honeygosky, vsc

All the fear of dying alone is there. But we need to go on. So we leave her, once again, - alone with her aloneness.

From there we go to an apartment where three elderly women struggle with the increased signs of age. They are sisters and laughingly, they joke about who is more sick; who is less weak; who is more in pain. Various stages and various forms of arthritis are what the doctor finds as she examines each in turn.

Then it's a block away to a room where a man with crippling multiple sclerosis struggles with his own helplessness. John is a man big in frame and all of his six foot six is one helpless burden to him. He can't walk and he can't sit in a wheelchair. So he lies there on his cot, day after day, month after month. He waits for us but he waits, - not just for the relief that the medication will bring during and after our visit. He waits because to him, we are a sign of hope. It is a moment that allows him to hope that maybe, just maybe, he will walk again. But he's both crippled and blind. And the prognosis is that he

About Ordinary Folks Who Said We Can: & They Did

will never walk or see again. But we leave him with his hope and we speak only words of encouragement. Somehow though, we both know that which we leave unspoken.

The next lady we visit, age ninety-six, is really fortunate. Mary has just recovered from a touch of pneumonia and tells us that daily, she feels stronger. She's just so glad we helped her recover from the pneumonia. And we are glad, too.

Next we stop by to see Rose, age ninety-two. She doesn't respond any more. Her unmarried son lives with her, and in his own unskilled but very caring way, he keeps his mother warm and dry and spoon-fed. Some liquid medication is prescribed for an infection that is in evidence. And then we leave. The son is glad that we visited, but we all know that this time, - his mother didn't even know we were there.

Mary, age ninety-three, is simple and childlike. "How long will I have to stay in bed?" Stay until morning and then we'll decide about tomorrow. But it's always the same directive, every tomorrow. For Mary has lay in bed, off and on, for ten years of todays and tomorrows. Mary's pain is gone now. Hers is now a morphined cancer without pain and, for Mary, it's just a few more tomorrows to lie in bed and then a whole new life for her, somewhere in forever, will begin.

Miss Arcessia Williams didn't want much. "Ah'm just fine. Jus' got to live with this misery." After her blood pressure and vital signs are checked, and medication prescribed, we chat a bit, leaving Miss Arcessia chuckling heartily in her wheelchair near the window as she returns to reading some long outdated magazines.

Our last stop this afternoon is with a man whose unmedicated hypertension resulted in stroke. He's listening to the baseball game when we arrive. As he grabs onto the enabling strap that hangs above his bed, he strains to hear whether it's a foul or a strike. We turn the radio down and ask how he's doing. It's tough. There's pain. Maybe I can get braces and learn to walk again. Maybe, we reply.

About Ordinary Folks Who Said We Can: & They Did

Just maybe you can. His wife, his only caretaker, has cancer. And we can't help wondering how either of them finds the courage to go on. How long can they go on, alone or together?

This is how F.O.R. incarnates the gospel a bit on a Saturday afternoon in McKees Rocks where in a territory of three square miles, there are four hundred bedridden elderly whom we know by name.

There's Leona McCalla and Rose Olenick and Frances Shearer and Ann Taucher and Vivian Layman and Steve Gerlosky and Bill Arbanas and … .

A WORD ABOUT HUMANITY IN PROCESS; IN HISTORY

"When is all this going to end?" many people ask, "or shall we be struggling forever?"

Part of the struggle will end this week, this month, in a year or two, or "sometimes, we hope" - according to the nature of the problem or the intensity of the crisis. But another part of the struggle will never end because it is partially caused by every person in the world-neighborhood learning to heal its brokenness and become whole.

Crisis life situations is but one aspect of this struggle. Crisis within self is its interface. Every self is engaged in resisting public and private oppression and in healing broken reality. Self struggles to become liberated from negative forces, both external and internal. For all, it is a lifelong struggle

So the word of peace has to be spoken; a stance must be maintained, and a continual her-story or his-story lived by each person. This word and stance - her story / his-story - is about the search for that notion and experience of freedom that says that no person is to be dominated by another, but that every person is equal and is a co-creator. It's a story that says that no person is to be imprisoned by anyone, or by any system. It's a story that says that every person is free to serve his and her brother and sister in peace. It's a story that says that every person is to design the best way to bring about the full experience of life's gifts; that every person is unique, self-determining, and is to be forever free from fear and oppression in this time/space world.

It is our deepest conviction that Wisdom will shine forth in the voice of creative persons gathered together in town meetings; that unconditional love is incarnated in creative servanthood, with neighbor serving neighbor; that we are forever developing within self and in our neighborhood that humanizing spirit, that encourages the full realization of the potential and zest for life of each and of all; and that no person shall have lived or died in vain, or lived or died unloved.

The future of F.O.R. rests with the leadership of its Director, Service Boards, By-laws, - its structures and strengths, - and with its dedicated staff and volunteers, its health professionals, its members and its supporters.

May Sto-Rox neighborhood experience and express the gospel of healing, and continue to foster human dignity through its servant and collective self, - the F.O.R. (the Focus on Renewal Sto-Rox Neighborhood Corporation).

APPENDICES

I. Summer of 1999.

To update this writing I visited the F.O.R. Center in the summer of 1999. In Rox Bottoms the flood gates are in place (and actually prevented flooding when the past year's Spring rains devastated several low-lying towns in northeast Pennsylvania); the oil tanks are gone, and the traffic pattern in Rox Bottoms has been changed according to the Flood Plan, that was originally proposed by the F.O.R. Citizen Committee.

F.O.R. dominates the landscape on the main street in the center of the town. The Senior Citizen Center, the Comprehensive Family Health Center, a Day Care Facility, a Job-Training and Literacy Program, the Senior Citizen Hi-Rise, and a fledgling Library are housed in buildings that line both sides of the main street of McKees Rocks.

I also saw several of the seventeen ACCESS transportation vans clearly marked F.O.R. as I drove through the town. The main street is no longer a thru highway. Route 51 traffic has been re-routed to streets on the outskirts of the town.

The F.O.R. Library, presently housed in the former Integra Bank Building, which was gifted to F.O.R. when the Bank relocated, has been approved for aid from the Pennsylvania Commonwealth Libraries. Its future is assured.

The Library is but another dream come true. One dream at a time has done so, - over nearly three decades of caring service. The controversial F.O.R. created in 1969, has become the town's center of hope and joy. Folks in McKees Rocks Boro and Stowe Township now proudly speak of "Our F.O.R."

And there's more. F.O.R. has recently set up a "twinning" relationship with Kazakhstan (a province of the Soviet Union until its collapse in1991). F.O.R. and Kazakhstan will grow and learn from each other through this relationship: a tribute to the gospel spirit of the people of Sto-Rox,

- very ordinary folks who said we can, and who did - locally, and now globally.

As Cardinal John Wright said when he dedicated the F.O.R. Center more than thirty years ago, "F.O.R. is for all the people of the McKees Rocks and Stowe Township neighborhood, regardless of race, sex, color, national origin, handicap, ancestry, age, religion, ethnic diversity or creed".

II. Summer of 2004

The Focus on Renewal Neighborhood Corporation, (F.O.R.), which over the years has brought a library, housing, family health center, ACCESS transportation for the neighborhood's elderly residents, a credit union, a farmers' market and other services to McKees Rocks, will soon add a Community Cultural Center.

The agency closed on the purchase of the former Desks Inc. Building at 420 Chartiers Avenue, on July 24, purchasing it for $258,000. (Old-timers will remember that the purchased building was once

Mayor Hershman's furniture store. Folks who tour it now are eager to see the "back room" where the Mayor and his cronies made that now infamous decision, - opposing F.O.R.'s unprecedented proposal that the federal and state human resource funds from Harrisburg and D.C. be awarded directly to the F.O.R. non-profit corporation, and by-pass the Mayor's office. F.O.R. won that initial battle with the Mayor, and then, as now, directly receives and well-spends several annual government human resource grants.)

Renovations will soon begin to bring the purchased building up to building code specifications, and to convert it into a center where art and ballet classes, and performances in music and the arts will be conducted.

The three-story brick structure, which had operated as a furniture store for seventy years, encompasses 22,000-square-feet and sits just across the street from the F.O.R. Sto-Rox Neighborhood Library.

"It's a great building," said Father Regis Ryan, F.O.R.'s current Executive Director. "It's in excellent shape. Everyone is amazed how well taken care of it is." He had praise for Elizabeth Jenkins Vos, the building's most recent owner.

"She was very kind to us; she brought the price down. And she was very patient with the process." F.O.R. hopes to have the Cultural Center open by next spring (2005). "We hope to begin offering music and art classes at that time for children and adults," he said.

Father Ryan foresees the Cultural Center as offering a full schedule of music, dancing, ceramics, arts and craft opportunities for young and old. "That's really a comprehensive picture of what we hope it will become," he said.

He also wants the Cultural Center to be a place where people can meet for coffee and socializing. Eventually, he hopes to also see an area in the building devoted to the sale of art works as a way to support and fund annual scholarships for local artistically talented youth.

F.O.R. has three Committees in place, made up of a total of thirty persons, who will oversee the Cultural Center development process. The Program Committee has been focusing on prioritizing the work, and designing the program content to be housed in the building. The Building Committee will oversee the renovations, both immediate and projected, and the Fund-raising Committee will seek financial support. "These three Committees are very enthusiastic and very committed to making the proposed Cultural Center work," Father Ryan said. "We've been discussing and moving on it for years."

The funds for the purchase of the building came from a Federal Community Development Block Grant, - awarded as part of the Sanders Task Force proceedings. "Seven years ago we sat with residents of several local housing communities in Sto-Rox to discuss the neighborhood's housing needs of the future," Father Ryan said. "Allegheny

County had entered into a federal consent decree to further integrate housing." The County had agreed to channel funds into seven area communities, which had been charged with disallowing any and all future housing discrimination, - in McKees Rocks, Clairton, Homestead, Braddock, Rankin, Duquesne, and Wilkinsburg.

"The residents decided that a Neighborhood Cultural Center would be a good thing to do," Father Ryan said. So we went to the Sanders Task Force and said, "This is what we want." After several meetings and prolonged discussions, the Sanders Task Force gave us a grant for $800,000 to be used to create a Sto-Rox Neighborhood Cultural Center."

The Committees had long been looking for a suitable site. "Finally, after seven years, we closed on the purchase of this building, which just came on the market one and a half years ago. It was in use until the day we closed on it," Father Ryan said.

The agency will now hire a program director, and will seek new means of financial support for the Cultural Center's operations. (As recently as August, 2004, the Heinz Kerry Foundation staff made an on-site visit to the Cultural Center. Given this visit, hope for operational funding may well be on the way. This is also true in that Point Park University Graduate students will do the research and help draw up the proposed budget request. Moreover, Point Park University has created a liaison position between the F.O.R. and the University, wisely appointing Graduate student, Patty Moran, to that position. Ms. Moran grew up in McKees Rocks, and as a child often visited and participated in the F.O.R. activities. Now she will enable other would-be organizers to come to her neighborhood, - to learn "About Ordinary Folks Who Said We Can: & They Did.")

Funding has been a continual challenge since Focus on Renewal began in 1969 as an effort to provide social services to the community's largely elderly and low-income population. The late Cardinal John Wright approved the proposal to create the Focus on Renewal program in the Neighborhood of McKees

Rocks and Stowe Township. Initially and for over a decade, Father Donald Fisher of the Diocese of Pittsburgh and Vincentian Sister of Charity, Sister Paulette Honeygosky, co-directed the implementation of the proposal for the Neighborhood F.O.R. Center. In the very beginning, all involved, - both staff and directors - were very dedicated volunteers, who laid the groundwork for the program's development and expansion under its present Director, Father Regis Ryan of the Diocese of Pittsburgh, and the Sisters of Saint Joseph of Baden, namely, Sister Ruth Bearer, Assistant Executive Director and Sister. Barbara Czyrnik, Assistant Executive Director.

F.O.R. has evolved, well beyond all hopes and dreams, into a sophisticated social service, neighborhood development agency with nine locations and a hundred fifty paid employees. Over several decades, it has transformed the former Equibank building into a Community Library and Learning Center; the former Union National Bank building into the agency's administrative office, and which houses the Credit Union, the ACCESS transportation service and a luncheon dining area for the Elderly; the former A&P store into the F.O.R.'s Sto-Rox Neighborhood Family Health Center. F.O.R. also began the Sto-Rox Plaza Hi-rise for seniors and a rehabilitated convent residence for the physically and emotionally challenged.

The F.O.R. Corporation serves some six hundred people each day through some twelve separate programs, including the health center, learning center, thrift store, transportation program, credit union and family programs such as Positive Parenting.

F.O.R. also began a farm stand two summers ago, bringing fresh fruit and produce to residents of McKees Rocks and Stowe Township communities on Thursdays from eleven thirty a.m. to two-thirty p.m. from May through November. The stand is located at the entrance to the McKees Rocks Plaza. The market helps nearby residents who don't own a car to now purchase a variety of nutritional foods,

- without having to take a bus or find a ride to more distant grocery stores. And, the farmers from Cambria County are able to sell all their fruits and vegetables locally. So, it's a *win-win* situation for the farmers and for the community.

"We keep growing; I'm not sure how," Father Ryan said. "Money gets tighter and tighter."

"It was a struggle when we were small and it's still a struggle, - especially with government funding getting tighter. But with each program effort, and especially through the Cultural Center, we hope to bring family values, education, music and the arts into the community." F.O.R. prides itself in being - through these many years - a Center "for all the people of the McKees Rocks and Stowe Township neighborhood, regardless of race, sex, color, national origin, handicap, ancestry, age, religion, ethnic diversity or creed".

III. The Services Created In The Neighborhood: 1965 - 2004

1. The Citizen Community Action Committee (C.C.A.C.), a politically active protest group, was formed.

2. This group (C.C.A.C.) wore two hats. It was also the Community Action Committee, (C.A.C.).

3. C.A.C. opened the federally-funded office of Economic Opportunity, and administered the federal human service programs in the neighborhood.

4. C.C.A.C. forced the first State-required comprehensive McKees Rocks Boro's Needs Survey to be done, and saw to it that the results were made public.

5. C.C.A.C. pressured the Public School System to publish its State-required Plan for Transition and its proposed Building Plans, which until this pressure group acted, had remained "secret". This led to several hearings at which the public could for the first time in

the town's history respond and react to the Plans.

6. C.C.A.C. succeeded in having Early Childhood Development Centers set up in McKees Rocks by the County Human Resources Department.

7. C.C.A.C. convinced the County Neighborhood Legal Service to open an office in McKees Rocks.

8. C.C.A.C. demanded that the School Board set up a comprehensive Adult Education Program within the Public School System. The School Board eventually did create such a Program.

9. C.C.A.C. also demanded that a Summer Recreation Program be sponsored by the Public School system. Again, the School Board did create the citizen-requested Summer Recreation Program.

10. C.C.A.C. brought the Carnegie Library Bookmobile Service into Sto-Rox, - at that time, a town with no library.

11. C.C.A.C. organized the town's first Nationality Festival that later became an annual event.

12. C.C.A.C. morphed into what was to become the F.O.R. Sto-Rox Neighborhood Corporation.

13. F.O.R.'s initial effort was to create the Child Health Center, which over the years has become a comprehensive Family Health Center.

14. F.O.R. organized Tenants' Councils in the four Housing Projects of Sto-Rox, namely: Terrace, Hays Manor, Uansa Village and Ohio View Acres.

15. F.O.R. demanded that the School Board set up a Parents' School Advisory Committee. It did.

16. F.O.R. convinced the School Board to begin a Lunch Program in the Neighborhood's Public Grade Schools.

17. F.O.R. and the local Presbyterian Church began a Meals on Wheels service for the town's shut-ins.

18. The F.O.R. Sto-Rox Neighborhood Corporation officially incorporated as a legal entity.

19. F.O.R. Inc. provided space for weekly Al-Anon & Al-A-Teen meetings. [It also at this time provides space for Narcotics Anonymous Meetings, and for the Mercy Behavior Health Services, which include individual, group, family and marital therapy for chemical abuse problems, co-dependency and adult children of alcoholics.]

20. After many meetings with the County, the need for a Mental

Health office in the neighborhood was established, thanks, in particular, to the support of Helen Tauber of Sewickley Heights, who served on the County Mental Health Board. As part of the negotiated agreement with the County, F.O.R. Inc. initially provided the office space for the County Mental Health unit that opened in Sto-Rox.

21. **In 1974,** F.O.R. Inc. developed and submitted a comprehensive **Senior Citizens' Service Proposal**. It was funded.

F.O.R. Inc. then opened a comprehensive Senior Citizens' Human Service office, and hired staff to implement the funded proposal. Rick Welsh, the Director, was well served by Co-Executives Kathy Woods and Nancy McBane.

Complementing that program, F.O.R. began a daily Senior Citizens' Group Meals Program.

22. **In 1974**, F.O.R. also developed a daily Senior Citizens' Transportation

Service. In the beginning, the transportation service was very simplistic. The "Anywhere in Town Bus Service", as proposed and voted upon at a town meeting, began with a volunteer, namely, Ed Demko, who would drive the F.O.R.-owned van four times a day around the town, making seventeen stops on each trip around. No fares were charged, but donations were accepted. The service was to operate only for a trial period, after which the program would be evaluated. If it proved to be successful, a full-time driver would be hired. The Assembly voted to spend a hundred dollars to finance the experiment.

Before this experiment ended, F.O.R. had developed a proposal, requesting a State grant to meet the transportation needs of the elderly in the neighborhood, and requesting two vans and funds to cover administrative costs. It was a happy day in 1976 when the two new vans were delivered to the Center, and there was money in the budget for two fulltime drivers and a fulltime administrator. It was the beginning of the seventeen van countywide ACCESS service now administered by the F.O.R.

The ACCESS transportation program, administered by F.O.R. under the competent direction of Ms. Lee (Liliosa Macadangdang) and with four fulltime drivers, transports the elderly in Sto-Rox to and from any place in Allegheny County on any weekday. A van is also available during evening hours, on Saturday morning, and to Church services on Sunday. In 1976 one van driver made nine thousand trips. In 2003, the four drivers logged more than 30,000 trips.

Sto-Rox residents over age 65, or those who are physcally challenged are eligible for the service. Transportation is also provided for persons of all ages in the community who use the F.O.R. Learning Center classes; the Health Center services; and the Positive Parenting programs.

23. **In 1974** at the Eighth Community Town Assembly, a motion was raised as to whether or not to create a **community-based credit union.** Would such an

institution more adequately meet the credit needs of the residents? Would it not provide the entry of thousands of people into the mainstream of financial services? A community-owned credit union could allow many of the poor and homeless to open an account and cash their checks, to take out a loan to buy a car, to send a child to college, to bury a family member, etc. Most banks consider persons on welfare too great a credit risk. But a community-owned credit union could take that risk. When the discussion ended, the motion was put to the vote of the quorum at the town meeting, and was approved.

The motion also authorized the staff to seek out neighborhood credit union experts like Father Geno Baroni for advice on how to secure capital investments in the credit union. (At a subsequent meeting, Baroni advised that we first ask the more affluent in the neighborhood and in the nearby suburbs to become substantial, no-interest depositors in the credit union. These deposits would then become the start-up capital loaned to, and then repaid by the needy, who would borrow and then repay the money.)

In the months that followed the July, 1974 town meeting vote of approval, F.O.R. Inc. established a federally-insured Neighborhood Credit Union. To this day, the credit union remains one of the most widely used services of F.O.R. But when it was initially formed in 1974, with a staff of unpaid volunteers and $200 in total assets, it was so very vulnerable.

It was originally housed in the storefront F.O.R. Center where it did not have the visibility it needed to grow. So, once again, at a town meeting, - a motion was made to relocate and expand the Credit Union. The plan was to move the Credit Union into a front street location (to the old CCAC office on Chartiers Avenue). That office space was so tiny, it had once been used as a janitor's supply room. But it was on the front street and that was important.

The plan also was to hire two part-time workers at a hundred and twenty dollars per month for one year. One part-time worker would take care of the books, and receive deposits and payments. The other would be an outreach worker in the community and take responsibility for securing new members and collecting delinquent loans. (Alberta Sutey and Mary Jones served their neighbors well in each of these roles.)

The rent was $15.00 per month. Utilities were extra. Salaries plus rent and utilities would amount to approximately $3,000 per year.

The Board of Directors of the Credit Union would include a person from each of the twenty-one block neighborhood units. Its various committees would be similarly organized.

Also, the President of the Credit Union Board would be *ex officio* a member of the Corporation's Board of Directors.

The Credit Union Committee had at their own Board meeting agreed with this plan, and had asked for the Town Meeting's vote and approval. The motion was voted upon and was approved.

The relocation plan worked. By February, 1980, the F.O.R. Sto-Rox Credit Union Board was able to announce that the Credit Union had assets worth $126,000. This was a very commendable record of growth and achievement in a poverty neighborhood.

Today the Credit Union, now housed in the F.O.R. main office building at 701 Chartiers, has a membership of 497, and it has assets totaling more than $380,000. Deposits are accepted in any amount, at any time. Withdrawals and loans are available upon request. Payroll deductions can be arranged. Savings are insured up to $100,000.

At this time, this credit union is primarily used to send the neighborhood's youth to college. The loan payback rate is more than ninety percent. And that is remarkable.

24. January, 1975. F.O.R. Neighborhood Corporation, and the F.O.R. Sto-Rox Health Council, added a Dental component to the Child Health Center. (The first chair was donated by a soon-to-retire dentist in Carnegie, who had heard of the need for dental care for the children of the Neighborhood.

The chair was a bit of an antique. Max Nieman, a volunteer electrician, worked through the night to put it together and get it to work. It served in good stead for a year or two, - until a proposal for dental equipment was written and federally funded. Two dental rooms with the best and latest equipment were then set up on the First Floor of the F.O.R. Center.)

25. January, 1975. Doctor Ron DiCarlos, a dentist for children, began working in F.O.R's Dental Care Room with Virginia Brennan as his assistant.

26. June, 1975. The first C.P.R. class, taught by Pat McMahon, was held at F.O.R. in an effort to educate for a volunteer fire department.

27. August, 1975. F.O.R.'s Minor Home Repair Service for Senior Citizen homeowners in Sto-Rox was begun, and was directed very ably by Phyllis Seibert.

28. December, 1975. The Food Buying Co-op became mobile because of a gift of a step-van from the local Presbyterian

Church, - a local Church that was always a good friend and benefactor of the F.O.R. Center. Ed Demko became the first of many volunteer drivers. In the beginning, the energy behind this effort was that of Felicia Kiesnowski. Ed and she would go to the produce yards, very, very early every Monday morning. Felicia knew she had to get the best price for whatever she purchased so that the cost to the elderly, served by the travelling Food Buying Co-op, could remain a bargain price. She always managed to get the farmers at the produce yards to keep the price low, and to gift a crate or two of their best produce to the "cause".

Returning to McKees Rocks with the van full of fresh fruits and vegetables, the van driver with a seller (different volunteers for each day of the week) would drive the van along a pre-set route, and on each corner where it parked, the elderly would be waiting; walk through the step van, and would buy their produce for the week. It was a twelve months a year, door-to-door service and was much appreciated by the town's elderly, especially those who were no longer able to walk to the grocery stores. At these block stops, the van driver and the neighbors on the street would also fill orders that were telephoned in to the block captains, and then would carry the groceries to the homebound on the Block, who couldn't walk to the van.

The volunteers who worked this program were a truly "hardy" lot, (Helen Tarantino and Joe come immediately to mind),and were difficult to replace on days when some personal conflict prevented their being on board for a regularly scheduled run. Also, by the fall of 1985 it was costing too much to keep the van in good shape. There was just not enough funding or enough volunteers to keep the program going. So this service eventually had to be discontinued, but not before Sister Jan Franklin, a recent addition to the staff, took charge of the Co-op and gave it a good six months more effort.

Rather fortuitously, as this program closed, the downtown regional Pittsburgh

Community Food Bank was formed.

In 1980, F.O.R. became a member and is a regular receipient of the Pittsburgh Community's Food Bank's largesse of surplus foods from the Department of Agriculture. Even to this day in 2004, F.O.R. continues to purchase canned and boxed goods from the Food Bank at ten cents a pound. F.O.R.'s food bank supply is further supplemented with regular food contributions from some of the local churches and grocery stores.

This food, stored in what was once the vault in the Union Bank Building and which now is the F.O.R. -owned Senior Citizen Community Center, is then given to those in need in Sto-Rox. The Food Bank in the vault is but one of five emergency food pantries set up around the neighborhood. Residents are served by the food pantry nearest to their residence.

In addition, the W.I.C. (Women, Infants, Children) food program is offered in the lower level of the Family Health Center.

29. February, 1976. A doctor for Senior Citizens, Dr. Lee, a geriontologist, began to practice at the F.O.R. Health Center.

30. March, 1976. F.O.R.'s newly-arrived geriatric nurse practitioner initiated an ongoing diagnostic health test program for the elderly.

31. December, 1976. A $25,000 Federal Community Development Grant was awarded to F.O.R. to be used to remodel and put in place the much needed ramps and rails, both inside and outside the Senior Citizen Center.

32. September, 1977. It's a long story, best described as the result of a "backroom" political decision, F.O.R.'s comprehensive Senior Citizen Service Program was in crisis for lack of funds. To keep the Center open, the experienced

Senior Citizen Staff (including its doctor and nurse) went on unemployment and continued to work. Due to their willingness to stay on, a modified service program remained operative while the F.O.R. staff struggled to regain the lost County-administered State funds.

Other volunteers, under the very caring and competent direction of Kay Koger, made hearty vegetable or chicken soup daily, and served it with crackers or wonderfully textured homemade bread, - a substitute for the full course meal previously served at lunchtime at F.O.R., - but which was yet another dimension of the program for which the County-controlled State funds were lost.

33. June, 1978. Eight months later, F.O.R. opened a Family Health Center when H.E.W (now known as HHS) awarded F.O.R. with a grant of $65,000 Federal funds, together with a medical staff of fulltime National Health Service Corps personnel (NHSC). Doctors John Platt and Bruce Bender came on board. (These funds by-passed the County; they

were State-controlled Federal funds, and the award was made directly to F.O.R., - and did not allow for any possible interference on the part of the County or the local politicians.)

34. June, 1979. The following year the Family Health Center was expanded when $195,000 was awarded to F.O.R. The National Health Service Corps now on staff included two internal medicine doctors, a pediatrician, a nutritionist and a second fulltime dentist, Dr. Stephen Pruce. (In addition to routinely developing an adult dental practice at the Center, there were a few brief ventures into dental care for the elderly homebound. One incident that stands out is that of Dentist Steve Pruce making an emergency house call. In the midst of a thirteen inch snow storm, a homebound elderly woman, who lived alone, phoned the F.O.R. Center in desperation. She was experiencing a great deal of pain from a throbbing tooth. "Is there any way we could help her?", was her question. When the message was given to Dr. Pruce, -

without hesitation, he said. Where does she live? I'll go to visit her. And, with his assistant, Virginia Brennan, as his guide to her home, wearing high boots and a borrowed heavy coat, he made a dental house call. It was service, - way beyond the call of duty.)

35. September, 1979. The four parochial schools in the neighborhood merged to form the McKees Rocks Catholic grade school. There was no other way for any one of them to survive.

36. June, 1980. The Family Health Center expanded further when half a million dollars was awarded to F.O.R. The grant covered a National Health Service Corps staff of two internal medicine doctors, a dentist, a nutritionist, a geriatric nurse practitioner, a pediatrician, health aides Rose Smarra and Elaine Herbst, and several outreach workers. All were fulltime staff.

37. December, 1980. A fulltime CETA Worker, sponsored by the County Hunger Action Coalition, began working at F.O.R.

She served as an advocate for a School Breakfast Program that one day would become part of the school system. It did.

38. January, 1981. The Rox and Stowe Firemen finally gave up doing Ambulance service when a Regional Ambulance Service was begun. This is an improved service, but it is a private and for profit business, and has close investment ties with many of the town's elected officials. It will need to be closely monitored.

39. In 1981, Additional Staff & New Energy. In 1981 Sister Ruth Bearer, CSJ joined the Center as Associate Director. In 1988, Sister Mary Lisowski, SC replaced Sister Ruth as Associate Director for one year. In 1989 Sister Barbara Czyrnik, CSJ joined the staff as fulltime Associate Director, in which capacity she continues to serve.

40. In 1985, the Learning Center was created. Through their daily contacts with hundreds of residents, F.O.R. identified

many adults who could neither read nor write.

Research regarding the demographics of Sto-Rox indicated that 53% of the adult residents had never finished high school. The State testing data further indicated that in the elementary schools, reading was a serious problem. Children who were learning to read had little help from their non-reading parents.

Aware that the ability to read is at least one of the skills needed for employment, and believing that the ability to read enhances self-esteem and self-empowerment, the F.O.R. staff set about the task of developing a Literacy Program.

In 1985 a request was made to the Pittsburgh Diocesan Campaign for a Human Development grant to buy needed books for tutors and students. When F.O.R. received $3,000 from the Diocese for this purpose, the Sto-Rox Literacy Consortium was formed. Its members represented education, financial institutions, social service agencies, fraternal organizations and religious groups. The consortium met monthly to discuss possible solutions for the literacy problem.

An area-wide appeal was made for additional funds and for volunteer tutors. Less than a year later, GED classes were added to the curriculum, and individuals in their late teens to their late seventies began to enroll in the F.O.R.-sponsored Graduate Equivalent Diploma program.

When an application for federal monies was made through the Women's Educational Equity Act, the Center received $36,000 to develop a "demonstration model" literacy program. Its major objective was to encourage female high school dropouts to consider re-entering the work force.

Through the relationships they formed in the G.E.D. and the Literacy Programs, it was hoped that the "women students", in particular, would begin to value their potential to become more productive members of society.

When federal funding for this type of program was cut drastically in 1987,

F.O.R. was able to get State funding. Over the years this State money was regularly supplemented with donations from local organizations. The paid staff remains small, but the number of volunteers continues to grow. Neighbors, who can read or type or do math, volunteer to teach those who cannot.

During the first four years of the Literacy Program, directed by Betty Cybator and housed in a building that around town soon became known as the F.O.R. Learning Center, about ninety women and men received their G.E.D diplomas. The youngest graduate was eighteen and the oldest was seventy-nine.

42. By 1988, The Award Winning Positive Parenting Programs were well underway. Early on, F.O.R. Inc. had created the "L", - a cultural, educational, recreational program for children living in the Hays Manor Housing Project. ("L" translates loving, laughing, living, learning) It was something of the

beginning of the comprehensive Positive Parenting programs and services offered by, and through the F.O.R. Center and presently so very capably administered by Amy Cetrone, the Program Director.

"Time Together", a drop-in center for moms and children which started in 1984, was initially housed in the basement of the original F.O.R storefront, - after the Health Center moved into the F.O.R.-owned Union bank building across the street. The Federal government, through the Public Health Service Program, provided the funds for the needed baby-proofing, child-friendly equipment, furniture and program funds. (The program also receives annual grants from the Heinz Kerry and Mellon Foundations, Children and Youth Services, and the County Mental Health Agency.}

The Positive Parenting Program was next developed. The purpose of the Positive Parenting Program is three-fold: to prevent child abuse and neglect in families identified as high-risk; to improve parenting skills, and to provide emotional support for parents struggling to cope with the stress of child rearing. Formal and informal parenting classes, counseling sessions for parents and a drop-in center are provided. Staff includes a parent educator, a nurse, and a social worker. The social worker primarily does the home visiting but staff members also make home visits, as needed.

By 1988, three hundred and sixty-five families used one or more of the Positive Parenting services. Especially popular were the classes in pre-natal care. In the fall of that year, Dr. Mark Richards, Pennsylvania Secretary of Health, recognized the worth of the Positive Parenting Program at F.O.R. and presented an Award of Excellence from the Department of Health and Human Services to F.O.R. and to the Positive Parenting Program Director, Mary Caruso.

Early on in the next year, 1989, the Positive Parenting Program opened Tot Time Drop-In Centers, well-equipped with toys and books, in the Hays and the Terrace housing projects, where kids and moms could enjoy recreating with each other in bright and happy play and learning rooms.

At this time, complementing the Positive Parenting Programs is the Butterfly Garden Early Learning Center, directed by Cyndi McAleer, and the Family Foundations Early Head Start Program, directed by Jennifer Caruso.

43. 1989, Housing for the Elderly.

In keeping with its commitment to the elderly, F.O.R.'s staff dreamed of building a senior citizen hi-rise. As early as 1976 a proposal to sponsor a McKees Rocks Senior Citizen Hi-Rise had been submitted to the Boro Council by the F.O.R. Staff. Not surprisingly, the Boro said "NO". It already had "too many tax-free housing projects". At the time it did have two, namely: the Hays Manor and the Uansa Village housing projects.

F.O.R.'s first formal attempt "to build it themselves" began with the formation of the Sto-Rox Neighborhood Housing Corporation on July 1, 1983. At that time the Center purchased property on Chartiers Avenue adjacent to the present

Health Center parking lot. The money was obtained through donations. The process of putting together the pieces for the hi-rise proposal moved slowly. After many lengthy discussions with the staff of Christian Housing, it was agreed that F.O.R., together with the Saint Francis de Sales Parish, apply for Housing and Urban Development (H.U.D.) Section 202 funding (which is given to private, non-profit groups to create housing units for low income residents who are sixty-two or older, and to create housing for emotionally and physically challenged persons between the ages of eighteen and sixty). The "Sto-Rox Plaza" proposal submitted to H.U.D. requested funds for the building of a hi-rise, and also funds for converting a vacant convent on the same street into housing for the emotionally and physically challenged.

In September, 1987, F.O.R. received word from H.U.D. that the "Sto-Rox Plaza" - the construction of a hi-rise for the elderly and the renovations of the convent to house the emotionally and physically challenged - would be funded. And that

H.U.D., through the Rental Assistance Program, would continue to subsidize the Plaza housing.

It was another dream come true. ... Two years later, in September, 1989, the elderly moved into the brand new hi-rise, and the emotionally and physically challenged moved into the renovated, former convent building. More than two hundred adults were home at last - not in an isolated facility in an isolated area of some town, - but on the main street of their own hometown. What a happy moment! Particularly so in that, among the well-wishers gathered to celebrate the opening event, were many new friends, who formerly were F.O.R.'s "political enemies".

IV. Significant Events And An Ever-Expanding Local and National Recognition of the F.O.R. As An Effective Neighborhood Development Model

August, 1973. Senator Mark Hatfield visited F.O.R. He praised F.O.R, calling it a model for neighborhood self-development. Subsequently in a report to Congress, he cited F.O.R. in the Congressional Record, Fall,1974, as a model to be emulated nationally, when he introduced his Neighborhood Self-Government Bill.

December, 1974. Fr. Donald C. Fisher was transferred to Africa. It's hard to explain, but F.O.R.'s Founder and Director, moved by the Spirit to take up the task of first evangelization, left F.O.R. to serve as missionary in Tanzania, East Africa. (On his first visit to the F.O.R. Center eighteen months later, he described the joy he experienced when, sitting at the base of a tree, encircled by Tanzanian youth, he told the story of the Resurrection. As he did so, a teen at the edge of the circle, wide-eyed and astonished, and who had never before heard this gospel story, said, "He rose from the dead? He did!")

February, 1975. Staff presented the F.O.R. Model for Neighborhood

Development to a group of professional organizers gathered on the Aquinas College campus in Grand Rapids, Michigan.

April, 1975. Al Julius came with a TV crew to F.O.R. Mayor John Kyle had been invited to the F.O.R. Center. But he refused to come to listen to the plight of the town's senior citizens. After waiting three hours for the Mayor, Al Julius did a two night series on the F.O.R. and its struggle to help the town's elderly. Al Julius' bottom line was: "Someday the Mayor will be a Senior Citizen and his Mayor won't come to listen to him."

May, 1975. Sister Paulette and the F.O.R. Corporation Board went to Washington, D.C. to give a presentation on the F.O.R. Model before the Alliance for Neighborhood Government. whose membership consisted of organizers from all fifty-two states. It required an all night drive to Washington, and an all night drive back, - but it was an exhilarating, learning experience, - well worth the effort.

May, 1975. Father Regis Ryan was appointed Director of F.O.R. by Bishop Vincent Leonard. Excellent choice, but the F.O.R. Sto-Rox Town Assembly reserved the right of approval. Only after sixty days' experience of his leadership, the town hall assembly said, would they officially vote him in or out as Director of the F.O.R. Center. (This empowerment thing knows no limits.)

July, 1975. F.O.R. staff again went to Aquinas College in Michigan to make another presentation.

July, 1975. Six busloads of happy Sto-Rox Senior Citizens spent the day at Cooper's Rock in Morgantown, West Virginia.

September, 1975. Thanks to Felicia Kiesnowski and Ann Podnar's no-interest loans, the Neighborhood Corporation was able to purchase the Union National Bank

Building (701 Chartiers Avenue) in which to permanently house the Corporation's services and town meetings.

November, 1975. F.O.R. staff prepared and presented a Case Study, entitled A NEIGHBORHOOD'S STRUGGLE FOR FREEDOM, to Theologians and Political Scientists gathered in Conference in Washington, DC.

December, 1975. F.O.R. relocated from the rented 610 Chartiers Avenue storefront space to the Corporation-owned 701 Chartiers Avenue across the street. Though it was snowing and ice-y, the residents and staff literally walked F.O.R.'s desks, books and chairs across the street. The town's main street traffic obliged the foot traffic by starting and stopping as needed. The move went so well that Christmas dinner, two days later, was served to the town's Senior Citizens at F.O.R.'s new location in the Union

National Bank Building. It was a citizen-effort triumph!

January, 1976. Very soon after the relocation from the rented storefront to the newly purchased building, Bishop Vincent Leonard came to Sto-Rox and re-dedicated the new F.O.R. Sto-Rox Community Center at 701 Chartiers Avenue.

April, 1976. The Child Health Center was the next program to be relocated from the basement of the storefront at 610 Chartiers to the second floor of the 701 Chartiers building.

March, 1976. F.O.R. was featured in the Parade Magazine, a Sunday insert carried in many national newspapers.

May, 1976. A Senior citizen trip was made to Moraine State Park (a simple pleasure too long denied to too many of the elderly in the neighborhood).

June, 1976. An Institute on Neighborhood Development was held at the F.O.R. Center. It was attended by the women religious of the Diocese with the hope of creating interest in this type of ministry.

August, 1976. Father Regis Ryan and Sister Paulette presented the F.O.R. Model at the Institute of Man and Science in New York.

September, 1976. At the County Building in downtown Pittsburgh, the town's Senior Citizens, with Ella Oliver in the lead, demonstrated to regain the federal funding for their much needed neighborhood services. (The funds had been taken from the McKees Rocks elderly poor served by F.O.R., and given to the affluent elderly in Stowe, who gathered primarily for social activities at a politically-controlled senior recreation center.)

January, 1977. Many folks pledged financial support when they learned that the F.O.R. had lost its senior citizen service grant. Encouraged, F.O.R. continued to serve the elderly on a very limited, shoe-string budget.

April, 1977. Sister Paulette received the Allegheny County Bar Association's Liberty Bell Award for demonstrating outstanding ability in developing services for senior citizens.

April, 1977. A presentation of the F.O.R. Model was made by Father Regis Ryan, Sister Paulette and several Board Members at the National Federation of

Priests' Councils Conference in Louisville, Kentucky.

May, 1977. F.O.R. sponsored a Senior Citizen day trip to Camp Trees (canes, wheelchairs and all).

May, 1977. F.O.R. staff and Board Members attended a three day Town Meeting in Avon, Massachusetts. The people of Avon opened their homes and offered gracious hospitality to the visitors, who came and who wanted to experience firsthand how government by town meetings takes place. We did. And we heard each other exclaim as we drove back to McKees Rocks : it does work. It can work. All told, it was a truly great people-development moment!!

October, 1977. Maggie Kuehn, Gray Panther leader, visited F.O.R. She saw for herself the grave injustice and negligence that had resulted in the town from decades of irresponsible (and corrupt) local government. Ever after the visit, she was an advocate on the national level for the elderly served by F.O.R.

October, 1977. Father Regis Ryan, Sister Paulette, Harry Mackey, Ann Podnar, Betty Cybator, Audrey Gross and Felicia Kiesnowski attended the National Gray Panther Conference in D.C. - at Maggie Kuehn's invitation, - where the staff made a presentation about the work of F.O.R.

November, 1977. St. Cyril's, a local parish, gifted a traditional Thanksgiving meal to the Senior Citizens, who regularly gathered at the F.O.R. Center for lunch. It was a generous and much appreciated gesture.

December, 1977. In a recent Allegheny County Study, F.O.R.'s comprehensive service program was cited as a model by the Hunger Action Coalition.

December, 1977. Gray Panthers sent Christmas Dinner and holiday treats to F.O.R.'s near four hundred daily lunchtime elderly.

February, 1978. Father Regis Ryan and Sister Paulette were invited to address the Business and Professional Women of Mt. Lebanon on the topic: "Is there no Justice and Caring for the Elderly Poor?"

June, 1978. The Third Street Neighborhood Park, long-awaited and much needed, was completed.

June, 1979. F.O.R. hired an engineer to do a study of the Third Ward Sewer problem. It was completed and is on file as the Widmer Study.

September, 1979. Father Don Fisher returned from Africa to become Director of the Bloomfield-Garfield Neighborhood Corporation.

October, 1979. The post-flood Agnes ' 72 Redevelopment Program in the Rox

Bottoms was completed. As facilitator, Sandy Wolf served her neighbors well.

December, 1979. Father Tom Shaffer, home from a seminary in Africa where he was on the faculty, worked as a summertime volunteer at F.O.R.

December, 1979. Reporter Vince Leonard of the Pittsburgh Post Gazette did a feature story on F.O.R.'s ten year effort.

January, 1980. Len Woods, home from Christ the King Franciscan seminary in New York, came to F.O.R. to volunteer for several months, thanks to Father Dan Lanahan's suggestion.

January, 1980. The Pittsburgh Press featured F.O.R. in its magazine section.

January, 1980. The Pittsburgher magazine interviewed the F.O.R. staff and did a story.

February, 1980. The Pittsburgh Presbytery, in preparation for the approval of a grant to F.O.R., asked the F.O.R. staff to make a presentation about F.O.R. at the Cathedral, - before Marguerite Hoeffer and the funding Board.

February, 1980. A Family Planning policy crisis surfaced at the F.O.R. Health Center. It was resolved amicably, but F.O.R. lost one of its finest pediatricians, when she challenged a long-standing F.O.R. Health Council policy. (It was hard to lose such a fine doctor, but the Board held to its directive that parents of teens seeking health care be involved in the decision-making that the situation might require.)

March, 1980. Father Don Fisher, always remaining a willing friend and consultant to the F.O.R. staff and its Service Boards, was appointed Pastor at a parish in East Hills, Pittsburgh.

March, 1980. The Norwood and Davis parks in Stowe Township were completed.

March, 1980. F.O.R. celebrated National Nutrition Day by setting up a nutrition office and a nutrition telephone counseling service. Also, special menus were on display for the day (with give away samples). The celebration was designed by F.O.R.'s newly-arrived National Health Service Corps (N.H.S.C.) nutritionist. The service has continued to expand and now includes individual and group nutrition counseling, and one-on-one assistance with meal planning, budgeting, and purchasing wholesome foods.

March, 1980. For a second time that year, F.O.R. opposed the Boro's unauthorized bank loan and requested a hearing in Harrisburg. The Boro borrowed $650,000 from the Pittsburgh National Bank without the required Department of Community Affairs approval. In a four hour hearing in Harrisburg Father Ryan served as F.O.R.'s lawyer. At the end of the day, F.O.R. won. The Boro's loan was blocked and its borrowing power will now be forever closely monitored by the State.

March, 1980. F.O.R. scuttled the Boro's band-aid, but costly Sewer Plans, and moved the issue to a public hearing and to greater scrutiny by H.U.D. officials and, as always, by the media.

March, 1980. F.O.R. mailed eight thousand copies of the F.O.R. newspaper, in its attempt to give the residents a full report on the progress on the sewer development issue.

July, 1980. A picnic for the neighborhood was held on F.O.R.'s parking lot. It was rained out but was quickly moved indoors, and ended up as a very successful community-building effort.

September, 1980. The Sto-Rox High School addition and renovations were completed by the district. (The tax burden that a new school would have created had been successfully avoided.)

February, 1981. Sister Paulette left F.O.R. and went to Chicago. There was a great deal of publicity, pro and con;

to some, she's a maverick; to others, a Mother Teresa.

February, 1981. Father Regis Ryan continued on as Director of F.O.R.

May, 1981. Sister Pauette and Father Ryan were invited to Philadelphia to receive a Federal Outstanding Service and Achievement Award for the work being done at the F.O.R. Center. Sister returned to McKees Rocks and was guest for the day at the F.O.R. Center. Then she went on with Father Ryan to Philadelphia to receive the award.

V. The Power Struggle Continues ...

November, 1973. The Home Rule Question was on the ballot. in Stowe and Rox. The people did vote Yes to the referendum. But the political machine's candidates, not F.O.R.'s, were in the majority on the Home Rule Commissions. Neighborhood Corporation members on the Study Commissions were a minority of two: Patricia McMahon and Georgene

Verlinich in Rox; Ann Podnar and Charles Ciamocco in Stowe.

November, 1974. At this election, F.O.R. worked to get the vote out and defeat the machine-written Home Rule Charters on the ballot. The Charters written by the local politicians, and not by the citizens as it was hoped they would be, had to be defeated. They were. The vote for the Charters was a resounding NO.

December, 1974. An attempt to close F.O.R. was made by the Mayor of McKees Rocks. Mayor Kyle, exploiting a brief moment, when Father Fisher left for Africa and had not yet been replaced, went with several other politicians to visit Bishop Leonard to request that the F.O.R. Center be closed. "No," said the Bishop. End of story. A bit of a crisis, but F.O.R. remained open.

January, 1974. A second attempt was made to close F.O.R., - this time by the firemen. A month after the Mayor's visit to the Bishop, the Rox Firemen took their petition to Bishop Leonard insisting that Sister Paulette be removed from F.O.R. Why? After considerable research F.O.R. had begun an effort to place a referendum on the ballot to determine whether or not the people wanted a volunteer, trained fire and ambulance department, - or, - did they want the untrained one they had, paid for by ever-higher taxes. The Bishop's response to the firemen: a referendum on the ballot is basic to a legitimate democratic process. F.O.R. remains open, and Sister Paulette stays.

January, 1975. A third attempt was made to close F.O.R. A "dumb", as in "not politically astute" clergyman stationed at a parish in Stowe Township, was urged by the politicians to go to the Bishop and apply for the position of directorship of F.O.R., and to operate the program out of a parish in Stowe. (Pragmatically, this would have led to the closing of the F.O.R. Center in McKees Rocks.) The following day the Board members and Staff of the F.O.R. went to Bishop Leonard to discuss the matter. The clergyman from Stowe was not appointed. The F.O.R. Center remained open, and remained where it was needed much more, - in McKees Rocks.

March, 1976. A petition to place the Home Rule Referendum on the ballot in Stowe Township was filed by F.O.R. It was F.O.R.'s second attempt to do so. It was challenged at the County level by Mr. Al Caputo, chairman of the Sto-Rox Democratic Party. It was subsequently rejected by the County Board of Elections, based on technical errors in the petition. F.O.R. admitted to the technical errors. (The referendum petition had been hastily prepared and, admittedly, there were errors such as the incontrovertible fact that a few folks had signed the petition twice, etc.)

May, 1975. A non-neighborhood park was to be built four miles outside of Rox in Kennedy Township for the residents of McKees Rocks. It was successfully blocked by F.O.R. at the award ceremony in the County Gold Room. Sister Paulette asked the H.U.D. officials, present at the ceremony, to hold back the award until a public hearing could be held. Before the television cameras the H.U.D. officials promised that such a hearing would be held and that they would be present to hear what the residents had to say.

July, 1975. The voting quorum in the by-laws of the Neighborhood Corporation was changed from 10% of the membership to 100 members. The ever-growing membership made this change necessary. It made the quorum count more manageable.

August, 1975. Sister Paulette was arrested (the first of seven times over eleven years) at the Rox Boro meeting. The Chairman said she could not speak because she was not a resident of the town. When she continued to speak and continued to question the misuse of federal funds for the elderly by the Boro elected officials, she was removed from the meeting room by the police, and she was subsequently arrested.

October, 1975. Senior citizens filled the room in Common Pleas Court where Sister Paulette legally sought her constitutional right to speak at public meetings (and won). [There was a moment in the courtroom that was intensely moving when, with the Judge, police and the politicians looking on, the senior citizens, themselves in need, took up a collection to defray Sister's legal expenses. Lou Loughren took the case pro bono. The money collected by the senior citizens was turned over to the F.O.R. lunchtime soup fund. Nonetheless, the collection courtroom drama received good media coverage.)

November, 1975. The Home Rule referendum for the second time was successfully placed on the ballots both in McKees Rocks and in Stowe Township.

November, 1975. Rox Council voted that the neighborhood park (now that a public hearing had been held and H.U.D. had laid down the law) would be built on a lot near the Middle School in the center of the neighborhood. Another citizen victory!

June, 1975. James Mollica, Stowe Township Commissioner, personally attended the County Hearing, where he opposed F.O.R.'s request for a grant of $25,000 from the County's Community Development Funds. (The grant would have been used to provide ramps, rails and other safety features in the Senior Citizen Community Center.) The power struggle had become that overt and upfront.

February, 1975. The Rox Council voted No to the construction of a Title II, Section 8 Senior Citizen Hi-Rise, advocated by F.O.R. (A decade later F.O.R. succeeded in having such a residence for senior citizens built. It is now owned and operated by F.O.R., - and is located on the main street of the town.)

May, 1978. Many homes of the elderly in the Third Ward were flooded. F.O.R. called in the Health Department and H.U.D. Also, the media were called in to photograph a few flooded homes, - for a "show and tell" in the newspaper and on the local tv news.

March, 1979. Hearings on the flooding problems in the Third Ward were conducted by the County. The residents were factually prepared for the Hearing by F.O.R.'s engineer. The Hearing allowed the residents to address the years of gross neglect of sewer repairs on the part of the Boro. The improvement of the sewers was now one step closer to reality. The media coverage and Mr. Widmer's study definitely helped.

Summer, 1979. There was more rain and more flooding of the basements in homes in the Third Ward. Citizen pressure on the Boro and the County increased proportionately.

December, 1979. A new problem: the Boro again borrowed monies without proper State authorization. The loan interest would increase the tax burden on the homeowners. So F.O.R. took the Boro to Common Pleas Court and was successful. The Boro's borrowing power is now held in check by the Courts. (With each such victory, the resistance to F.O.R. by the politicians and those whom they control with jobs and housing and perks also grows.}

October, 1980. A Sewer Improvement Plan was approved by the County. Approximately 3.7 million dollars will be spent to improve the sewers in the Third Ward in McKees Rocks. The funds will be 80% County-received-Federal funds; and 20% Boro - received Federal funds. Construction will begin in March, 1981. The F.O.R.-Widmer Plan was not selected, but it served its purpose as a catalyst for the decision that was eventually made.

January, 1981. At a town meeting, it was decided that the Home Rule Question would be placed for the third time on the May ballot in McKees Rocks.

March, 1981. Mike Sprys, Boro Councilman and candidate for Mayor in May, was held for court on charges of selling near seven million dollars worth of hard drugs in Sto-Rox.

May, 1981. On election day, the Home Rule Referendum, for the third time, was on the ballot. The result was a Yes vote and a bit of a victory. But, once again, on the Study Commission, F.O.R. had only a minority voice. [Over the years, for the voter, it was very confusing. First, we asked the voters to vote Yes to the Home Rule referendum on the ballot. In the subsequent election, we had to urge them to vote No to the Charters for Home Rule that were written by the elected officials' reps on the Study Commission.

The next year we asked them to vote Yes on the referendum, which they did, - but the elected officials had printed the Study Commission nominees on the ballot in such a way that it was hard to figure which persons were the F.O.R. representatives, and which were the elected officials' representatives.

Surprisingly, the electorate took each attempt, failure that it was, in stride. For them, it was a win-win situation all the way. They became an increasingly savvy voting public. At the end of it all, it can only be hoped that they now understand that on every Election Day, - their vote, each vote, really does count.)

So it is and will be that F.O.R., having educated the Neighborhood's voters, will continue to speak out, and will continue to outperform a local government that long ago has forgotten that it is to be a government, - of, by and for the people. Perhaps, one day soon, even they,- will remember ….

Those persons, who would replicate the F.O.R. Development Model in their own neighborhood, might reflect upon the following:

That, in every neighborhood:

The Priortizing of the Needs-To- Be-Addressed
Is To Be Local,
Based On A Door to Door Grassroots' Listening & Organizing Visit.

The turf needs to be manageable (block by block meetings, followed by town meetings).

And though the Approach May Be Both Creative & Unique,

The Principles Of Governance -
To be Servant Of, By & For The People -
Are Universally True, Always and Forever.

Through it all, remember that it takes a lot of "neighboring" and "putting faith in practice"
to heal a Neighborhood,
and to make a Neighborhood "holy", "whole", and "wholesome".

About the Author

Paulette G. Honeygosky is a world traveler and scholar. She was educated at Duquesne, St. Louis and Bonaventure Universities. Honeygosky has also worked extensively as a teacher, a human rights activist and advocate for the elderly.

Printed in the United States
32033LVS00004B/35